BARBARA

BARBARA

The Laughter and Tears of a Cockney Sparrow

by

Barbara Windsor

with the assistance of
Joan Flory

CENTURY

LONDON   SYDNEY   AUCKLAND   JOHANNESBURG

Published in Great Britain in 1990 by Century
An imprint of Random Century Ltd
20 Vauxhall Bridge Road, London SW1V 2SA

Century Hutchinson Australia (Pty) Ltd
20 Alfred Street, Milsons Point, Sydney, NSW 2061, Australia

Century Hutchinson New Zealand Ltd
PO Box 40-086, 32-34 View Road, Glenfield, Auckland 10, New Zealand

Century Hutchinson South Africa (Pty) Ltd
PO Box 337, Bergvlei 2012, South Africa

Set in Monophoto Apollo by
Servis Filmsetting Ltd, Manchester

Printed and bound in Great Britain by
Mackays of Chatham

British Library Cataloguing in Publication data
Windsor, Barbara
        Barbara: the laughter and tears of a cockney sparrow.
        1. Cinema films. Acting. Biographies
        I. Title
        791.43'028'0924

        ISBN 0-7126-3519-X

To my mother, who loved me though I didn't always know it

Preface

When actors have to cry on stage, some can just turn it on like a tap. Others, like me, have to find things inside themselves, the worst things that have happened to them in their own lives.

In my case one very vivid scene is always ready to push itself to the surface.

I was woken by a knock on the door. That bloody postman, I thought. I've told him, if there's any registered post, leave it till the second post. Blue padded into the bedroom. He put his front paws on the bed, towering over me. I checked the clock. It was five o'clock. Ronnie turned over drowsily. Wearing only my dressing-gown, I slipped out of bed and downstairs. When I opened the door the floodlights hit me – it was like walking on stage.

Outside the house were police cars, tracker dogs and men armed with guns. They must have switched off their engines and run their cars silently down the gradient in the road.

'We've got a warrant for Ronnie Knight.'

As if I didn't exist, they swept in. They were everywhere. The ones who went for Ronnie took the stairs two at a time. I remember feeling strangely calm as they searched all the rooms, in cupboards, drawers; I saw one of the men scraping dust from the bottom of a wardrobe and putting it in an envelope.

'Ssh, don't wake my mother,' I said.

'Don't worry Barbara, we'll be gone soon,' said a

policewomen.

While all this was going on, Ronnie came downstairs under escort. He was dressed, but by the look of him he hadn't been allowed to wash or shave. They made him sit helpless and forlorn as they continued to turn the place upside down. When they'd helped themselves to photographs, diaries, papers, they led Ronnie away. He said, 'Don't worry, Bar, it'll be alright. Just phone Jimmy'.

'We suggest you call your solicitor, Barbara,' said a policeman.

It was 16 January 1980, the day I had intended to break the news that I was leaving Ronnie for good.

1

I was going to be a boy. That's what my mother had set
her heart on. She made lovely blue baby clothes in
preparation for the great event. Imagine her surprise on 6
August 1937, when out pops little Babs. I'm not sure
Mummy ever really forgave me for not being a boy.
Needless to say, Daddy was pleased as punch, not least
because the little bundle already bore a striking
resemblance to him.

They called me Barbara after the nurse, and Ann
after an ice-skating star, Barbara-Ann Scott. So there I
was, Barbara-Ann Deeks, seven pounds of joy.

The doors were never locked in Angela Street and all
us kids used to play in the cobblestone street. You seldom heard a car, it was mostly the coalman or the rag-
and-bone man with his horse and cart. Whenever the
rag-and-bone man appeared, all the kids would scuttle
indoors to fetch empty jam jars. Washed clean, they'd
fetch a halfpenny to buy sweets from the corner shop.
Rags as well meant a goldfish.

Our house was always spotless. The smell and the glow of Mansion polish was as familiar as the hopscotch patterns chalked over the pavements. The front doorstep was scrubbed every day, whatever the weather. Each family had a zinc bath, usually brought into the kitchen and placed in front of the boiler where I'd be given a good scrub down after a boisterous day's play.

In the outside loo the newspaper was cut into neat little squares, threaded with string and hung on a nail. They knew how to treat the tabloids in those days!

My mother, Rose, was pretty and petite with lots of curly red hair. Looking good was important to her and anyone close to her had to look presentable too, otherwise they'd be letting her down. She was always anxious to better herself, go up in the world. She hated Shoreditch, where we lived – *too common*. She was a skilled seamstress, made all her own clothes and most of mine.

Daddy was a typical Jack-the-lad Eastender, brought up in Flower and Dean Street within earshot of the hustle and bustle of Petticoat Lane. He had a barrow, selling fruit and veg. He was dead handsome and full of fun. You could see why she fell for him.

He loved the East End and its people. He was always whistling, so nobody ever knew what kind of mood he was in. His lack of ambition and unwillingness to move from Shoreditch caused many squabbles. It beat me why he ever married Rose. They had so little in common, apart from dancing. The war brought things to a head.

I was two years old, too young to be evacuated with other children. Daddy received his call-up papers and joined the army. We gave up our home in Angela Street and

Mummy and I moved in with her parents, Nanny and Grandad Ellis in Stoke Newington. Their small house in the Yoakley Road already accommodated two families. Uncle Charlie Windsor, Aunt Dolly and their son, Kenny, were downstairs with my grandparents. My mother's brother Ronnie, too young for call-up, had the upstairs back room; Mummy and I had the front room. It sounds like sardines, but actually it worked very well. Aunt Dolly attended to the house, saw to Kenny and looked after me. Mummy went to work, and Nanny did the cooking.

Nothing much happened in London after war was declared; life went on much as normal. Many of those evacuated returned home. Then on 7 September 1940, at five o'clock in the afternoon, London had a shock. Three hundred and twenty bombers and six hundred fighter planes came roaring up the mouth of the Thames. Their target was the docks. Buildings in the hinterland were flattened like a pack of cards. Londoners were dazed and confused. Many panicked and left the city again. The next night, 8 September, planes came over at eight o'clock in the evening and kept up the bombing till four in the morning. Over a thousand people were killed and not one German plane lost. The blitz went on for 57 consecutive nights.

I found it all exciting. I loved seeing everyone scatter when the throaty sound of the air-raid siren built up to a crescendo. There wasn't always time to get to the street shelter. Mummy always dived under the table. 'Babs, Babs, quick, get under the table,' she'd shout. Then at the whistling descent of a bomb, she would clamp her hands over her ears, chin dug into her chest, waiting for the explosion. Sometimes I'd just stand there laughing. I got many a slap that way. To me it was all a game – kids have little sense of danger.

I had one special friend at school, Margaret. Every morning she'd sit on a wall at the top of Yoakley Road, waiting for me. There was always the excitement of looking over the previous night's damage. We'd often turn up to school with scuffed shoes after clambering over the debris. Then one day she wasn't there. She had been killed by a piece of flying shrapnel while waiting at our usual meeting place.

After that Mummy was determined I should be evacuated as soon as possible. I made a fuss at first. I was a war baby. Bombs, guns, fires, were part of my life. But when the time came to go, dressed in a little bonnet and coat, clutching a small brown case, I boarded the train as good as gold. I was bound for Lancashire, though no one knew exactly whereabouts. Coaches awaited evacuees at the other end, but someone told me to get into a private car because the house I was going to in Blackpool would only take one child.

From the word go I hated the home I was allocated. There was a man and a woman. I was only five but I knew straight away that *they* were up to no good. I was made to undress in front of them. Mummy had told me never to talk to strangers, yet here was a man always coming into my bedroom and trying to touch me up. I took to barricading myself in my room, pushing heavy pieces of furniture against the door to stop them getting in at night. I just used to scream if either of them came near me, and I'd cry myself to sleep. My only wish was to get away as soon as possible. I wrote home:

Dear Mummy,

I don't like it at Blackpool. The food is rotten. I get cold potatoes. I know there is a war on but I don't think it's fair. If I have bread I can only have bread with jam and bread with marge. I don't think they like me 'cos I come from London. They all talk funny up here. Come and get me soon.

Love, Babs

PS. The airplanes fly very low here.

I was always a bright kid with a well-developed imagination. My mother found me once, outside in the street in my nightie, looking up at the night sky. 'I wonder what it's like to sit on a star,' I said.

'Don't be daft,' she said. 'Just my luck. Why can't I have a daughter like all the other kids?'

Evidently Mummy now thought this letter was my vivid imagination at work again and chose not to take any notice.

I was at school in Blackpool with a little girl called Mary North. When she told her mother about the evacuee who cried all the time, the woman investigated. She reported her findings to the authorities who discovered I was billeted with a brother and sister posing as man and wife. The last I saw of these people was the police taking them away.

I moved in with Mary and her parents, Uncle Henry and Aunty Flo. I was very happy there. We used to go out to the countryside, a new experience for the Cockney kid. I'd never seen frogs and tadpoles before. I remember, too, watching Aunty Flo making sweets.

They were round, like Maltesers, and covered in white powder. Some mint, others toffee.

For all the comfort and security of being with the North family, I must have been a bit of a tearaway. Aunty Flo wrote to Mummy:

Your daughter is obviously used to playing in the streets. I can't do anything with her. When she comes back from school she eats her tea and goes straight out again. If you agree, I intend sending her to dancing school.

I was with the North family for nearly a year until something happened to change everything. One evening I was out walking with Aunty Flo, when in the headlights of an approaching bus I saw a couple canoodling. The shock of the lights made the man look up. It was Uncle Henry.

'Look Aunty Flo, it's Uncle 'Enry, kissin' and cuddlin' that lady,' I piped up, innocent as the day is long.

When we got home, Mary and I were sent straight to bed. But the rumpus downstairs kept me awake. Feeling guilty, I decided to go downstairs and apologise. 'I'm sorry, it's all my fault,' I began, but I never got any further, because the anxiety overcame me and I fainted.

Now Aunty Flo couldn't wait to get rid of me, and I was put on a train to London. Back home, when I told her what had happened, Mummy gave me a clout. Some homecoming!

It took ages for my Lancastrian accent to wear off. The first day back I said at the tea table, 'Willya pass t'boota please, Moomy?' and they all burst out laughing.

'Say something else, Babs, go on.'

I burst into tears.

Our house was one of the luckier ones in Stoke Newington, still standing in the huge open spaces where buildings once stood. Nanny Ellis, who was the sweetest lady you could meet, was so petite we used to call her Little Nanny. She had a beautiful air of calm and love about her. I wished Mummy had more of Nanny's sweetness, but I suppose the war made her hard. She always had an independent streak, an unwillingness to conform to the tightly-knit society of the East End.

Aunt Dolly looked after me while Mummy went to work. She was my favourite aunt. She was very fragile, and the only one of the grown-ups who didn't go out to work. Although she was also very strict, I could talk to her as I never could my mother. In fact I was always good as gold with Nanny and Aunt Dolly, but the minute my mother came home I started playing up.

Grandad Ellis was the epitome of a Cockney man — hard-working, warm-hearted, witty and generous, too, despite the poverty he'd known most of his life. His shift at the docks was from early morning to lunchtime, which meant the pubs were still open when he finished. At closing time he'd stagger off the bus just as we were coming out of school. Mummy told me I must walk on the other side of the road and ignore him. She didn't like me seeing him tiddly. He'd sing songs like *My Ol' Man* and *Are Soles Lovely*. Mummy hated anything coarse. I always waited for him, though. He'd give me tuppence to buy a jam doughnut or threepence for a quarter of sherbet lemons, my favourites. Mummy caught us one day and hit me all the way down the street.

Once, when I was in bed, suffering from measles,

Mummy came in from work and stuck her head round the door. 'I'll just have something to eat, Babs, then I'll come back again.' That wasn't good enough for yours truly. I wanted attention and I wanted it NOW. The minute she got downstairs I banged on the floor. I banged even harder when I heard her say, 'Oh, leave her.' I shouted, 'You'd better come now or I'll hit you with a big stick.' That fell on deaf ears, too. It was only when no sound at all came from the bedroom that she came to investigate. When the rest of the family heard her shouts, they rushed up the stairs. There I sat in the big bed with a cherubic face covered in spots, a pair of scissors in my hand – tufts of hair were everywhere and what little I had left was all jagged and spiky.

After D-Day everyone thought the war would be over in a matter of weeks. Mummy wanted to move into a home of our own again in preparation for Daddy's homecoming. She fancied a prefab on a bomb site, but I wasn't so keen. Apart from anything else, it was where my friend Margaret had been killed.

A week after D-Day, London was under attack again, this time from Hitler's secret weapon, the doodlebug. Directly the sound was heard in the distance everyone stopped whatever they were doing and waited. As long as you could hear the engine, it was all right. Mummy used to shout, 'Keep going, you bugger, keep going!'

I cried buckets when Aunt Dolly died. There was an autopsy because her death was sudden, and poor Uncle Charlie was taken down the police station for questioning. They needed to find out if the poison found in her stomach had been wrongfully administered. An inquest decided Dolly had died of gastroenteritis as a result of eating some dodgy ice cream. As for poor Uncle Charlie, he came home a broken man. Already stricken with grief, the business with the Old Bill tipped the scales. He had to be admitted to a mental home. He remained as gentle and loving as ever, but the will to live left him after Dolly's death, and he died soon after.

It was a sad end to life in Yoakley Road. We'd all come through Hitler's onslaught unscathed, so it seemed like a cruel twist of fate.

Mummy and I moved into the prefab. Ours was the last of the row and had an enormous garden which backed on to a cemetery. Inside it seemed like a mansion, and I had my own bedroom at last. Above all we had a bathroom and inside toilet of our own – no more sharing.

Every other father came home, but because Daddy was in the Eighth Army, he was the last from our area to be demobbed. 'Your father's dead. He ain't coming home,' the other kids used to chant at me.

With Daddy away and Mummy out at work I was often alone. When I went next door to my friend's house to see if she could come out to play, I used to pray to God, 'Please let Pamela be in.'

Then, because I felt lonely, I was always getting into fights. What really got me going was when the other kids chanted, 'Your mother dyes her hair and earns ten pounds a week!'

Mummy often went up to the West End with her friends in the evenings, and she would come back with nylons and chewing gum.

One day I heard a familiar sound and I ran to the door. Daddy was coming up the path whistling *Nancy With The Smiling Face*. He handed me a bar of peppermint chocolate. 'Don't show the other kids. Put it in your pocket out of sight.' I ran off to broadcast the news that my Dad was home, but none of them believed me. I had no option but to produce the chocolate. 'See, he is home, *so there!'*

Daddy used to get cross with Mummy for looking glamorous. She was thirty-three then, very pretty and loved dressing up in the clothes she made herself. 'What are you doing in those high heels?' he'd say. 'You should be wearing brogues.'

My father had great difficulty getting a job after his demob. Young interviewers treated him like he was from outer space. They would say to him 'What have you been doing?' 'Fighting for the likes of you,' he'd say, 'I was in the bloody desert!' He thought they had no respect. Eventually Mummy went to an interview for him and got him a job on the trolley buses. I was proud of him in his uniform, driving the 647 route from Tottenham to Stamford Hill.

We spent a lot of time together. He read to me a lot. He talked to me, telling me about the concentration camps and the persecution of the Jews. He'd always lived among Jews – his wife worked for them. He respected them for their industry and endeavour, and the fact they had given employment to so many during the Depression. Yet even in the East End, anti-Semitism was rife. I can still remember Mosely and his blackshirts marching down Ridley Road – the screaming, the shouting and the fights.

Ironically, he nearly lost his job because of a Jew. Driving along the Dalston Road he got into an argument with a passenger. The man jumped off the bus shouting, 'You're only saying that because I'm a Jew!' That did it. Daddy was furious: 'I've spent the last five years trying to save you lot.' A threatening crowd of Jews appeared from nowhere. 'Why didn't you fight like that in Germany?' he shouted.

His impromptu stop caused havoc, messing up the entire electrical circuit. To get things going again, his trolley bus had to be forcibly removed from the rails by the engineers.

Rows at home were becoming more frequent – Mummy and Daddy really brought out the worst in each other – and Mummy's fancy clothes were often hurled into the back garden. My father was volatile and Mummy would seldom back down. Melodramatic, he called her. Sometimes she didn't speak to him for days.

My role was pig in the middle. Mummy always found something to pick on, usually my fine hair. She was forever spitting on it to make it curl and dressing it up with a big ribbon. One day in desperation she sent me off to the hairdressers for a perm. When she came to collect me, she went bananas. My head was covered with puppy-dog tails and they hadn't even bothered to remove my heavy coat and gloves so I was soaked with perspiration. I looked a fright!

Daddy was also strict at times. He was always picking me up on the way I spoke. He also had a thing about me sitting up straight. He'd thump me on the back if I slouched and say, 'Don't forget, the chest is the best thing on a woman. It's the chest that counts.' No wonder I grew up flaunting my boobs!

In fact I was a right little exhibitionist. I'd kiss any boy I could get hold of. Bus journeys were always an ordeal for Mummy. I'd hop of my seat and dance down the aisle, doing impressions of Betty Grable and Veronica Lake. I'd hitch my skirt up for Grable, and pull my hair over my eyes for Lake.

My school report read: 'She is above average intelligence, but she's too frantic. She must try to calm down.'

Dental care was always a big thing with Daddy; and he used to lure me to the dentist by promising a trip to the pictures afterwards. The first time I had a filling they took me to see the voluptuous Jane Russell in *The Outlaw*, quite daring for its time, and I made the mistake of mentioning it the next day in class. 'Your mother musn't take you to see films like *The Outlaw* – it's rude.'

'Not half as rude as *Duel in the Sun*, which I saw last week,' I said. Mummy was summoned to the school and given a right bollocking. I remember she flounced out, saying, 'I'll bring my daughter up how I like!'

But I loved Church Street School. No matter how naughty I was, I never seemed to get the cane. It was always the person next to me. Then I overheard one of my teachers say to someone, 'You could never hit her, she's too little.' My classmates on the other hand were always picking fights with me, probably because I liked showing off with my singing and dancing.

All the aggravation was better than being on my own, though. Because I was an only child I often used to turn up at school in the holidays to talk to the janitor and help him clear up. At other times I used to go and sit in the church and read the bible. I was the only kid I knew who hated the long summer holidays. My cousins, Roy, my dear godmother Aunty May's son, and Kenny never included me in their games. 'Go on, go away,' they would say. 'We don't want girls.' I was only allowed to keep *cave* while they smoked in the old air raid shelter.

I think Daddy worried about me being lonely.

'How would you like a dog, Babs?' he asked me one day. I was delighted and I promised my less-than-ecstatic mother I'd take good care of it. She made us promise we'd get a little one, but there was this beautiful Alsation called Tessa at the RSPCA. Mummy went spare when we brought her home and demanded we take her back the next day. I wouldn't eat or talk for two days. In the end Mummy couldn't stand it, and she let us fetch the dog back. She was the most wonderful dog, and even Mummy grew to love her after a time.

On Thursday nights Daddy took me to see his parents, Jack Deeks and Fat Nanny. My mother hated me going. She considered them common and a bad influence. Jack worked at the docks. He was tall and good-looking, like my father. Fat Nanny worked as an office cleaner. She reminded me of one of those wooden dolls with a pretty round face.

'Don't let her stand outside the pub when you go in for a drink,' Mummy used to say to Daddy; it was a common sight in those days to see kids hanging around outside the pub, sipping lemonade and nibbling crisps. But Mummy saw me standing outside Dirty Dick's once, and my father and I never heard the last of it.

Saturday night was party night. It was the pub first, then home for what we called a Dutch Auction. Everyone was expected to get up and do a turn. Mummy wasn't much of a performer, but she had a go. *Dapper Dandy Was a Very Funny Man* was her party piece. Daddy's contribution was usually *How Yer Gonna Keep 'Em Down On The Farm*. Needless to say, I needed little encouragement.

Grandad Ellis used to sit me down and tell me stories about the music hall and Marie Lloyd in particular. In his youth there were music halls all over the East End, and he'd seen all the great stars. He'd often appeared at the local drinking clubs, billed as 'The Versatile Comedian', singing and cracking jokes. He hoped I would go on the stage one day. On Sundays we'd go to Harrow to see Uncle Alf and my lovely Auntie May, my godmother, who was the most glamorous woman I'd ever seen.

I had no ambition then, but, as I say, I fancied the idea of singing and dancing, so I was sent to classes at Stoke Newington town hall once a week with Madame Behenna and her Juvenile Jollities. Madame Behenna had the same dimensions as Fat Nanny, but she spoke with a posh voice through half an inch of make-up. My first job was a show we did in Blackpool. I came back with a note from Madame Behenna saying: 'She's a born dancer. She must keep it up.'

Her pianist, known as Aunt Bessie, loved the songs of Al Jolson and as I sang them she made me imitate the way he used his hands. She taught me how to put a song over.

Having passed my 11-plus (with the top mark in the whole of north London!), I had the choice of three grammar schools – City of London, Skinners, and Our Lady's Convent, Stamford Hill. City of London was too far on the bus from Stoke Newington, Skinners sounded far too hoity-toity, so that left the convent.

'I must say for a little girl you've certainly got a lot of brains,' said the Reverend Mother at my interview. That decided it.

I announced I wanted to be a nun when I grew up. One day Mummy caught me swanning around the house with a tea-towel wrapped round my head and a sweet smile on my face. Hardly what she was used to.

I was something of a local star by this time, and she was less surprised and a lot happier when a talent scout called Brian Mickey, who was to discover Morecambe and Wise, spotted me in a charity show for Madame Behenna and asked if I'd like to join the Eleanor Beam Babes for a pantomime at Wimbledon Theatre. As soon as I walked through the stage door, ready for my audition, I forgot all about being a nun (sorry, God). I just knew the stage was for me.

But the Reverend Mother disapproved of the theatre and refused to release me from the convent for the two-week run. I became very depressed and truculent. Bloody impossible in fact. My mother was sent for and the Reverend Mother asked her to remove me from the school. As I was still only 13, I had to go somewhere that gave an all-round education as well as stage training. We were advised to try the Italia Conti School in Soho or Aida Foster's in Golders Green.

The walls at Aida Foster's were covered with glamour girl pictures, people like Jean Simmons, and Elizabeth Taylor. Aida Foster looked at me and said: 'She isn't what we usually have, but she's obviously got something'. Compared with the other pupils I had no *class*. Everyone spoke posh except me and my straight hair looked as if it had been cut round a pudding basin – everyone else had Shirley Temple curls. I may have been blonde and dainty, but I wasn't pretty in a conventional way. To make matters worse they sat me next to the gorgeous Shirley Eaton, who was to become famous as the Goldfinger girl.

The others would arrive in Rolls-Royces. I had to get three buses from Stoke Newington. When Daddy came to collect me in his bus driver's uniform, the others would all scoff. 'Ooh isn't he common,' said one girl, and I went for her, pulling her hair out in clumps. When her chaperone tried to pull me off I picked up a tin of face powder and threw it all over her.

The endless dancing classes worsened my complex about having little legs. Just a glimpse of myself in the wall-length mirrors, attempting *grande ronde des jambes* or an *arabesque*, was enough to spoil my day. All the other girls had legs up to their armpits. I didn't care for the acting classes either. It was dreary recitations in a posh voice. I felt they were trying to change my personality. Then one day we were told, 'just do whatever you like'. I chose to impersonate a French maid. I took a deep breath, stuck out the bum and the chest, and I was away! I went home happy for the first time that day. I knew I'd done well.

Aida saw I had talent and she gave me credit for my timing and my versatility. She was also an agent, so there was always the opportunity for us to perform before a proper paying audience. She used to put on a troupe at the Golders Green Hippodrome. I was put on the end of the line because I was the littlest, which meant I got to say the line 'Here come's the baron!', and was the only one who spoke.

The queue was a mile long at my first big audition. As the queue, which went round and round the Palace Theatre, got shorter, we could hear the girls doing their stuff. You could hear these squeaky voices trilling through the stage door, mostly doing *I Hear A Robin Singing*. Each time a man's voice cut them short, 'Thank you. We'll let you know.'

I didn't have the range to do all that trilling, so I did my own jazzed-up version of *Sunny Side of the Street*.

When I'd finished, he said, 'How refreshing! That's absolutely marvellous . . . now do an American accent.'

They needed fifteen-year-olds with loud voices, under five feet tall who could look like ten-year-olds. At four feet ten and loud as they come, I was just what the doctor ordered. I was to play Sadie Kate, one of the orphans, in a touring musical called *Love From Judy*, based on the film *Daddy Long Legs*, with Jeannie Carson, June Whitfield, Adelaide Hall, and Johnny Brandon.

I was ecstatic. Suddenly everyone at Aida Foster's wanted to talk to me. Little Barbara-Ann Deeks was a star in the making!

I was sitting in the auditorium one day and this really dishy, wavy-haired man walked across the stage. He introduced himself as Johnny Brandon. I held my breath. I was 15 years old and, for the first time in my life, I fancied the pants off a geezer. I thought he was the most wonderful creature. He had blond hair like my father's and was a very snappy dresser. He was very American in the way he walked, and when he got up to perform he had that raunchy, American-style projection and pzazz. I was very naive, I'd never had any sexy feelings to speak of before, but I used to pass his dressing room every night just to say, 'Good evening Mr Brandon' – but without stopping because I was too shy to talk to him face to face.

The older girls in the chorus were completely baffled by my crush. One of them said, 'I don't know why you're so smitten – he's queer.'

'Oh,' I said, 'isn't he well, then?'

She tried to explain what queers did, but it did nothing to put out my fire! Besides I scarcely understood what boys and girls did, let alone boys and boys. My crush lasted for two painful years.

Love from Judy opened in Coventry in the autumn of 1952 and went to Bournemouth and Birmingham before coming into the West End of London. It ran for two years and three months. A year into the show I developed a bosom. I'd grown it without noticing. All the other kids grew upwards, while little Babs grew outwards. The wardrobe mistress had to use a huge piece of elastic to bind my boobs. Mummy was furious I had put on weight; she was afraid I'd take after Fat Nanny. 'That terrible bosom,' she said. 'They're awful. You take after your father's side.'

Whenever I was asked my name at an audition, the reaction was always the same: 'Pardon? Wot? How do you spell it?' So Aida Foster decided I should have a stage name. I chose Windsor because it was Coronation year and because it was my Aunt Dolly's name.

Daddy got the hump about me dropping Deeks, and I think he worried I was growing apart from him. Mummy and Daddy were both proud of my success, but they were unable to share it because their married life was now in ruins. Blazing rows between them would send me rushing off to my bedroom in tears.

We moved from the prefab to a flat in Stamford Hill, but the marriage continued to disintegrate. It was six of one and half a dozen of the other. Mummy could be a real bugger. There was the occasional right-hander from Daddy.

Mummy's nerves were stretched to the limit. A divorce seemed inevitable, though neither of them ever discussed it with me.

I was on tour in Manchester when I was called back to give evidence at their divorce hearing. In court, the judge asked me if I'd heard their rows. I said I had.

'Have you ever seen Daddy hit Mummy?'

'Yes,' I said. I'd been brought up to tell the truth. I was still very young for my age and I just didn't understand what was happening. Maybe if I had, I'd have lied or said I wanted to be with my father.

Daddy was standing in court, listening, his face all flushed. They asked me to write down the swear words I'd heard him use. Then I was asked to leave. I was standing outside when the divorce was granted. When Daddy came out of the court he walked straight past me as if I were a stranger. He never said a word.

Mummy had been awarded five shillings a week.

When I'd finished in *Love From Judy*, I used to walk back along Daddy's bus route in the hope of seeing him. One day I'd done some shopping and his bus appeared in the distance. As it approached, I stood on the kerb, waving frantically. He saw me all right, but he drove straight on without a glance in my direction.

2

I had gone into *Love From Judy* with short hair, ankle socks and school uniform. I remember at the first dress rehearsal I had stood up and there had been blood all over the back of my lovely white dress. Some kind person told me it was perfectly normal, all part of growing up, but it frightened me to death. All my mother said was that I'd strained myself at exercise class, causing me to bleed internally.

June Whitfield said everyone knew when I grew up: one moment I smelled of carbolic soap, the next it was Chanel No5.

I approached the end of the show in 1954 with a bouffant hairdo, stockings and high heels. I was 17. My once-elasticated boobs were now unleashed on the world, all 38 inches of them! The fashion was for figure-hugging skirts and sweaters, and nipped-in waists. I desperately wanted to be fashionable but I wasn't prepared for the knock-on effect! As I teetered past building sites in my high heels, unable to conceal my newly sprouted arrivals, I'd hear: 'Allo darlin'. Seen yer feet lately?' followed by a chorus of raucous laughter. I was self-conscious and I hated it.

I also hated being at home. Mummy and I fought like cat and dog. I'd become a rival for reasons I didn't understand. Mummy didn't have a man now. She continued to say terrible things about the way I looked. Little Nanny said, 'The silly cow. She used to flaunt herself something rotten.' I didn't know what flaunting was. I knew nothing about sex or being sexy. My apparent exhibitionism was all totally unconscious. Mummy had always led me to believe I was a plain child, and at the convent, sex had not been in the curriculum. So nothing was said at home or school.

Towards the end of *Love From Judy* I landed a bit part in the film, *The Belles of St Trinian's*. I just had to lean out of a window and shout, 'Ta-ta, see you in the hols!' in my best Cockney accent. Mummy saw it as another act of defiance on my part. 'When I think of all the piecework I've done to pay for you to get rid of that awful voice,' she said after the screening. I could never do anything right for my mother.

My heart-throb Johnny Brandon gave me a beautiful necklace and bracelet as a farewell present at the end of *Love From Judy*. 'It's a raw talent you've got – I just know you're going to be a big star,' he said. I had great difficulty in getting Johnny out of my system. I sobbed endlessly. Mummy was so worried she took me to the doctor, who diagnosed puppy love.

A month later, Johnny sent a telegram asking me to appear in a sketch with him on the BBC TV variety show. It was a sort of Shirley Temple thing and we did the same sketch again in a television series called *Dreamer's*

Highway. Then we took a stage version of it on the road, opening at the Grand Theatre, Bolton. It was my first taste of twice-nightly variety.

On tour I felt very much alone. The dancers kept to themselves. I usually stood in the wings and watched the show. There was a young comic who did the last spot in the first half. He paralysed the audience with laughter. While he was on, a lady stood beside me with pen and pad, solemnly marking his gags out of ten, so that when he returned to that venue he knew what they liked. They say in show business you create your own luck. Well, Ken Dodd certainly did that. When we came on after him, we died on our arse.

The end of the tour signalled a bad patch in my life. I missed my father dreadfully and Mummy was even more miserable than I was. We needed money so I had no choice but to think of doing something outside the business. But there wasn't anything else I could do! Eventually I took a job as a sales assistant for seven pounds a week in Sherry's, an upmarket shoe shop in Edmonton.

By now I was beginning to realize what my bosom and bottom were for. Men always came in with their women, because in those days they always paid the bills. The 'in' colours were cherry, tan and sage green; if I sold a pair of shoes I had to push the matching gloves and handbag. These were kept on a shelf nearest the ceiling, so I worked out a cheeky routine. 'Oh sir, those gloves would look so lovely on madam.' I climbed slowly up the ladder, wobbling now and again. At the top I hovered provocatively, so the husband or boyfriend would get an eyeful. 'Perhaps I could interest you in the matching handbag! Feel this, genuine crocodile!'

It worked a treat. I took £90 on my first Saturday – a lot of money then. Believe it or not, this upset the manageress. From that day she really had it in for me, and I got the boot after the January sales of 1955.

Being out of work meant I had more time for friends. My best friend was Greta, who worked in Woolworth's. She wore too much make-up so, needless to say, Mummy disapproved of her and told me not to bring her home. Ankle chains were in fashion, so we adapted some old necklaces and wore them to our first dance at the Royal, Tottenham.

My other best mate at that time was Frankie Stephens, a fair-haired Jewish boy who I met at the Salt Beef bar in Stamford Hill. All these guys were ogling me when I walked in, and Frankie just came over and said he knew a friend of mine, and we started chatting. I could really talk to Frankie. He had an amazing mind. We had long discussions late into the night. It reminded me of talks I used to have with Daddy. We used to go dancing down the Empire Rooms and Frankie loved showing me off, his bubbly blonde shiksa, in front of all his Jewish friends. As soon as he went off to the loo, all these Jewish guys would descend on me like a pack of wolves.

One night I had my handbag stolen and Frankie never had any money, so we were stuck. I cadged a lift off one of these Jewish boys, and just as I was climbing into his car, I said: 'Can my boyfriend come, too? Quick, get in Frankie'. The boy said yes, but his eyes said 'Cheeky cow!'

Frankie used to say I didn't care about him and took him for granted, but I cared about him more than anyone at the time. We're still good mates today.

Life on the home front became a lot easier to bear

when my mother met Len Atkinson, who was divorced. They were married in the summer of 1955. She was so lucky to meet Len who was the sweetest of men. I took to him immediately, and he encouraged me in my career at a time I needed it most.

I was still turning up for every audition going, but I never seemed to get a foot in the door, let alone a chance to show 'em what I was made of! The break came when I caught the eye of writer Peter Myers, well known for his late-night revues, at an audition at the little Watergate Theatre off the Strand. It only held about 100 but it was an upmarket clientele, with lots of people from the business. The company for this revue included Jimmy Thompson, Thelma Ruby, and Edward Woodward. We did six weeks, and then I was held over for another show. I did more cabaret work at Monsieur Vincent's Côte d'Azur in Soho – now Ronnie Scott's club. There was a number entitled *My Hair, My Teeth, My Bosom* which I sang with Una Stubbs, the teeth, all sweet and innocent, a girl called Fifi, all raunchy with a shock of red hair, and yours truly, all bubble and bust! It was a riot.

Soho in those days was full of Greeks, Arabs and Maltese. They went mental for blondes with bosoms. I lost my virginity to a customer at the Côte d'Azur, a crazy rich Arab who wanted to whisk me away. He kept coming to the club to watch me strut my stuff, then sending me flowers and chocolates the next day. He was so extravagant. In fact I only went out with him because he gave me all these presents – I was embarassed. I remember going off to a party he threw for the whole cast in Westbourne Grove and coming home deflowered. 'Is that it?' I thought. The next morning what had happened that night was lost in an alcoholic haze.

'My God, he *did it* to me' I said to Georgia Brown.

'Well, you were asking for it,' she said.

Looking back, the real reason I'd let it happen was that I'd found out my boyfriend at the time, Albert Davies, had been screwing someone else. Since *we'd* never even done it, you can imagine why I'd got the hump, as it were.

My next boyfriend, Al, as I called him, was a vegetarian garage mechanic and motor cycle freak, my first proper boyfriend. He was very handsome, but his hands were always grimy from oil and engines, which put me off. Mummy, who was always a great one for judging a book by its cover, didn't think a mechanic was good enough for her Babs.

By this time, though, I was discovering boys in a big way, and having a steady boyfriend was not my style. Once I discovered sex, I assumed you just did it. Nobody told me otherwise! Once after the show one of the bosses asked me to go and sit out front with one of the punters. 'He'll give you a oner,' he said.

'I'm not a hostess!' I protested.

'I know you,' he said. 'You'll go off and do it with one of the musicians for nothing!'

Before my stint at the Côte d'Azur came to an end I'd met a young man who would have a big impact on my career. 'You're the best thing I've ever seen,' he said after the show, 'I'd dearly like to handle you!'

'I bet you would,' I said.

'No, really. My name's Peter Charlesworth; at the moment I'm a music publisher, but I'm thinking of setting up as a theatrical agent.'

Next time he came in with a friend who wanted to meet me, a young comedian called Benny Hill. We went back to Benny's for coffee and he told me how Peter had persuaded him to come along that evening.

'I've been to this club,' Peter had told him, 'and I've seen this little girl. She's so funny, Benny, you ought to see her. She comes out and gets everyone laughing. She's got great comedy timing, she can sing and dance, and Benny, you want to see her fucking knockers!'

I was working in another shoe shop in Holloway to pay the bills when Peter called me out of the blue to say that he'd left his job and was now a theatrical agent. He told me about an audition at Ronnie Scott's jazz club. Annie Ross was ill, and they wanted someone to replace her on tour. Ronnie Scott at that time had a small club in Gerrard Street, where I auditioned with six other girls who all had better voices than me. How I got the job I've no idea. I knew bugger all about singing with a band.

I had a long blue dress with forget-me-nots all round the bust. When Ronnie Scott saw it, he lifted his eyes to the sky. 'The dress is very nice,' he said, ripping off the flowers poor Mummy had stayed up all night sewing on, 'but these flowers are covering up the box office!'

Annie Ross was a big name in jazz then, but the punters didn't know Barbara Windsor from a packet of Woodbines. I could almost hear the squelch of rotten tomatoes as we went into our first number. Ronnie was great. He joined me at the microphone, stuck a couple of maracas in my hands, and we were away.

Travelling round the country in a coach with an all-male band is a bit hairy for a little girl trying to pretend she's grown up. I'd already lost my virginity and here were all these horny guys let off the leash. I was madly in love with Ronnie Scott, and guys like Tubby Hayes, Les Condon, Tony Crombie and Benny Green were my idols.

There was a lot of late-night knocking on my hotel door, followed by a little voice saying 'Sorry, I'm asleep!' Typical musicians, they thought I was fair game. In those two weeks with the Ronnie Scott Band I learnt more about men than at any other time. It was the first time in my life I'd gone off the rails. I loved the world and his wife after a few stiff G and Ts. At the end of the three weeks I went to see Peter. I had changed completely, my skirt hitched up, hanging out everywhere, chewing gum and sayings, 'Yeah man' and 'Right on!' Peter decided that that was the last time I would be allowed out on tour!

Back in London, I went into a terrible revue at Winston's, a new nightclub, with Fenella Fielding, Jill Gascoine, Barbara Ferris and Amanda Barrie. The club didn't take off, so we were given our notice. The night before it came off, I was invited to a party in Soho. I remember Di Dors was there. I kept knocking back the booze until I blanked out. Next morning I was relieved to find myself in my own bed, but my head felt like an elephant's arse. When I pulled myself together I realized it was Sunday. Whatever happened to Saturday and our final show!

I called Bruce Brace, the owner of Winston's, to apologize in a terrible state. He just burst out laughing. Apparently I had gone to Winston's, staggered on to the stage and proceeded to rubbish the show: 'Isha flop, thash wotitish,' I spluttered, 'I'll show yer 'ow t'do a proper show . . .' By all accounts, I took over the show and belted out a couple of my best numbers, *Sunny Side of the Street* and *You Made Me Love You*. After this all the customers said I should take over the show, and to my surprise, Bruce asked me to stay on at Winston's. That was when it all started to happen for me.

There was another club over the road called Churchill's and Bruce told me he wanted to poach one of their performers, a drag act called Danny La Rue. I wasn't sure about it, because it was my show at Winston's and Danny was so good, I thought he'd steal my limelight. Against my advice Bruce signed him up and in no time, Winston's was *the* place to be seen. Bryan Blackburn's material was outrageous – parodies of Diana Dors and Gina Lollobrigida and so on.

Danny and I soon became the best of chums. One night some guy yelled at me every time I came on stage: 'Woo darling – I couldn't half give you one!' etc. In the end Danny stepped in: 'Watch it, mate, or I'll be down to see you.'

'Yeah, get off, you old poofta!'

'Don't let this wig fool you,' said Danny, jumping down off the stage and whacking him one. After that, Danny adopted it as his catchphrase.

One day Bruce said: 'I've got this ice-making machine. Every table's gonna have a bucket of ice! That night there was a big party of lads from south of the river, and they started throwing ice onto the stage.

'If you want to see a fucking ice show,' I said, 'go up to the Empire pool.' It was that sort of club.

Ronnie Corbett was another Winston's protégé. I said to one of the hostesses one night, 'I feel so sorry for little Ronnie, he's always ligging about on his own.'

'You're joking.' She looked astonished. 'He can take his pick from us lot any night of the week!'

Just imagine, all these voluptuous ladies lusting after little Ronnie! He ended up marrying the very beautiful Annie Hart, one of the stars of the show.

Victor Mature was a regular visitor and even though

I'd been told he had the hots for me, I was silly and giggly when we were introduced. It was at a party full of debutantes who were crawling all over him and grabbing him. I remember that he picked up the phone to make a call and by the time he'd put the receiver down one of the girls had pulled his trousers off. 'Come and sit next to me,' he said. He turned to Tommy Yeardye, Diana Dors's lover:' Look at this little face!' he grinned. I stayed the night with him, but we never actually *did it*. How could I possibly have sex with this wonderful film star I'd seen as Samson when I was ten? It wasn't right. He phoned my mother the night after I'd stayed with him to say I'd left my earrings behind. She gave me another clout when I got in.

Three nights in a row I went out with Bing Crosby's son, Gary. He looked just like his father. He took me to all these posh hotels, like Claridges, which I hadn't been to before. On the last night he said 'Can I take you home?' We got in the taxi and I said 'Stamford Hill,' forgetting it was over an hour from the West End. When I got in I rushed up to Mummy and woke her up: 'Mummy, Mummy, I've been out with Gary Crosby!'

'Wouldn't have minded you waking me up if it'd been Bing,' she said.

I often used to go on to the Côte d'Azur for a drink after the show at Winston's. A talented young singer I'd heard about called Cliff Lawrence would get up to sing. He had a thin, hungry look I find very attractive. He was a natural with an amazing voice somewhere between Frank Sinatra and Mel Torme. Looking back on it, I think I fancied him because he was so talented; I think we all want to fuck talent whether it's Frank Sinatra, Elvis Presley or Michael Jackson or whatever.

Cliff saw me in the audience and asked to meet me. We started going out. People were always running him down and trying to discourage me from seeing him. He had a funny devil-may-care attitude to work and success and often failed to show up for gigs, using some allergy or other as an excuse. He was madly temperamental. In fact he seemed to be hellbent on destroying his career, what there was of it.

We were always fighting and I'd often turn up for work with a black eye or a bruised arm. He dragged me along the street by my hair once because I didn't want to go home after Winston's. He acquired gambling debts too. Once he forged my signature on a cheque that bounced. So eventually Cliff's behaviour started to affect me. I'd always been a stickler for getting to work on time, now I didn't bother. But there was another reason – I kept feeling sick.

'You're pregnant!' my mother said accusingly.

My mouth fell open. 'Don't be silly! How can I be?'

'We'll have to find somebody. You can't possibly have it.'

I had no say in the matter. Mummy simply took over. She sent me to some woman in Streatham. Straight in and out, twelve quid, no questions asked. Nothing'll happen for 12 hours, the woman said. So I trotted off to Winston's to do my usual spot. By the time I got home in the early hours of the morning I was in excruciating pain. I phoned the woman in Streatham, but she didn't want to know. Mummy shouted down the phone: 'My daughter is dying!' Then the woman told us what to do. Mummy sat me on a bucket of very hot water and gave me plenty of opening medicine.

Despite the trauma of that night, my mother still told

me nothing about sex or contraception. So a couple of months later, unbelievable as it sounds, I was going through it all again.

On my 21st birthday Cliff and I went to a party at a club in Knightsbridge with Richard Lyons, the son of Ben and Bebe Lyons. Richard adored Cliff's singing and he was surrounded by fans. He seemed like a god that night. When he asked me to marry him, I said yes. The next morning a picture of the three of us appeared in one of the daily papers, with a caption saying Cliff and I were engaged. I called my mother to tell her it was true. That was it. She'd always thought Cliff was bad for me and she'd done her damnedest to stop me seeing him. She told me never to come home again. So I'd know she meant it, she had all the locks on the doors changed.

Obviously we needed two incomes to afford our own place, so it made me so mad that Cliff kept performing for nothing. We were at the Nightingale Club in Gerrard Street one night when Cliff got up to sing. As usual everyone adored him so I said to the manager, 'Why don't you give him a spot?'

He was paid in advance, and the next day we went out and bought him a suit. That night I reminded him that it was my guarantee that secured this job. 'So don't you let me down,' I said.

'No, no, of course I won't, darling.'

Guess what? No Cliff. I could not believe it. I told the people at the Nightingale I'd go and look for him. Just as I was giving up I found him coming out of a drinking club at the bottom of Gerrard Street.

'How could you do this to me?' I screamed.

He was about to trot out the usual excuses when we caught sight of the Nightingale's guv'nor accompanied by two bouncers heading in our direction and looking distinctly unfriendly. We turned tail and ran but it was a waste of time in my high heels. They grabbed hold of Cliff. I knew he was in for a beating and I begged them not to. If they damaged his face, he'd be finished. I stood in front of Cliff and felt a beefy fist land on my smacker. The bouncers were mortified.

As they scraped me up off the pavement, Cliff made his escape.

Peter Charlesworth suggested I should audition for a role in *Too Hot to Handle*. It was Jayne Mansfield's first (and only) British film, built around her prized assets, and to make sure everyone got the message, they made her lean against a lot of walls.

Jayne asked me to dye my hair because she didn't want any other blondes in the film. But I refused because I was still in cabaret at Winston's and couldn't just turn up brunette one night. What with that, and the fact that my boobs were almost as big as hers, we didn't get off to a very good start.

I was meant to be playing a teenage girl from *oop north* who gets a job as a dancer in a London nightclub. But the director never told me what accent to use. I started off Northern, then went on to American. Nobody seemed to notice. They were only interested in promoting Jayne and her outsize boobs.

Cliff was still pestering me at the club but I was losing patience with him. It was true what they said about him, he was a messer. I decided to stop seeing him.

I started getting telephone messages at home from someone called Ronnie Knight. The name didn't ring any bells. Then I remembered. A few days earlier I'd been out for lunch with a mate, Neil, in Stamford Hill, when he said, 'Don't look, but there's a guy just driven past three times.' The car, a two-tone cream and grey Zephyr pulled in, and out stepped a stunningly handsome man in an immaculate double breasted grey suit and beautifully curled hair – I heard later he used to model at the local hairdresser. He said, 'Hullo Neil. How are you? Aren't you going to introduce me to this very pretty lady?'

Like all East End, men he had a way about him, a swagger.

Neil told me afterwards that Ronnie had never spoken to him when they'd been at school together, but he got in touch with him later to get my telephone number. When we finally spoke on the phone, he asked me out. I turned him down three times, because I was wary of going out with people outside the business – they tend to think we're easy meat. Besides, I don't like people coming after me. I like to make the first move. But he kept calling. Eventually he said, 'If you don't agree to go out with me this time, I won't bother you again.'

God knows why, but I found myself saying yes.

When he picked me up in his car I thought he was lovely. After a while he said, 'You dun'alf talk a lot.'

Later he said, 'Don't look at me when you're talking to me.'

'Why not?'

'Because of my nose. The first bit of money I get I'm going to get a nose job.'

And he blushed.

I was sitting with him after the show, and a girl kept leaning over him, making it plain she fancied him. When I came back from the loo, she was sitting next to him. I picked up my plate of Chicken Maryland and threw it at her, but it went over Ronnie. He laughed. 'You ain't half got a temper,' he said.

I'd had loads of boyfriends after Cliff who all wanted to marry me. They'd send me chocolates, flowers – one guy even sent me a dog! Going out with Ronnie was so refreshing after the extravagance of these show business types.

Mummy said, 'He's a dangerous one. Reminds me of your father. Good looking but a bit of a rascal.' I thought to myself – she only ever opens her mouth to criticize.

At the end of the first week he said, 'Will you do me a favour? Will you be a good girl over the weekend?'

'What do you mean?'

'They're all like hot cakes around you, and, well, I dun'alf like you.'

And he blushed again.

This was the start of Ronnie's jealousy. He was madly jealous from the start. He didn't like me showing off my boobs in tight sweaters or whatever. 'I know you've got a big bust,' he used to say, 'but you don't have to throw it around.' I wanted everyone to think I was the sexiest thing ever.

I think Ronnie expected me to be a virgin, but I knew all about sex when we started going out. He was quite naive, and there were lots of sexual things he'd never done. 'Gorblimey, how many times 'ave you done that?' he said, when I offered to do one particular thing for him. He stormed out, and I didn't see him for several days. He asked me then how many men I'd been to bed with, and he walked out again when I told him! After that I decided to keep mum. I decided it was unwise to try to talk sex with Ronnie. I even remember once telling him I liked jazz. 'It's dirty music,' he said. 'Don't talk about it.' All this was very difficult for me because it's in my nature to be upfront about things.

If Ronnie wasn't keen on talking about sex, he was certainly keen on doing it. It was all sex with Ronnie and me at the beginning. We just used to listen to 'Moonglow', which was our song, and make love.

Things were to remain good with Ronnie as long as the sex was good. Ronnie made me feel safe. I felt I'd always be alright as long as Ronnie was around. I'd never been so happy.

One lunchtime Ronnie was at Mummy's flat. I was cooking him a meal (I wanted to show him how domesticated I was) when the phone rang. It was my old flame, Cliff Lawrence, screeching down the line like a demented parrot, making threats about how he'd expose me to the papers. He said, 'You've got someone there. I'm gonna shoot him.' He said he was in a phone box nearby. Ronnie grabbed the phone. 'I'll see you round the corner!' No sooner was Ronnie out the door than he reappeared. 'What does this geezer look like, Bar?' So we jumped in the car and both went looking for Cliff – except I had no intention of letting Ronnie find him in case he did Cliff some damage. I knew Cliff would stand no chance with a heavy guy like him. I saw Cliff hiding in a telephone box, but I just let Ronnie drive on by.

Just as everything with me and Ronnie seemed hunky-dory, when I'd realized I'd fallen madly in love, I got an anonymous phone call saying he was a married man, with one kiddie already and another one on the way. I was devastated. How could the bugger do this to me? When I had it out with him he just laughed: 'What difference does it make? It all happened before I met you.

I'm going to marry *you* now.' Honestly, can you believe the cheek of it!

Soon afterwards I found out I was pregnant again. I tried to call Ronnie but he seemed to have done a bunk. Next day I discovered he'd been nicked. I felt sure it was a case of mistaken identity. I didn't really know what Ronnie did for a living. He'd told me he bought and sold things. Street trading is how many East Enders earn their crust – I didn't question it.

At the court hearing, a mutual friend pointed out Ronnie's wife, June, a pretty girl, heavily pregnant. Ronnie was released on bail.

That night I gave him a right earful. I'd seen another side of Ronnie Knight in the dock, flash and arrogant. He'd looked bored and shown absolutely no respect for the law. He'd looked at the judge with an expression that said: 'You're wasting my time, you stupid old prat.' 'If I'd been the judge I'd never have let you out on bail,' I said.

'Look, Bar, I am innocent,' he said, adding, 'if I am found guilty, you must finish with me, okay?'

At the trial Ronnie got 15 months for receiving stolen goods. Under the circumstances I decided the best thing for everyone concerned was for me to have an another abortion.

It was ten o'clock on a Saturday morning, a few days after Ronnie's conviction, and I was at the stage door of Wyndham's Theatre, about to do an audition. I was still feeling choked about the case and I didn't even want to be there. Inside the stage door, under the dingy light of a brick passageway, I could make out the vague shape of a podgy lady in a woolly hat.

'What do you want?' she asked.

'I've come about the audition.' Then I found myself thinking out loud, '. . . but I'm not really bothered to be honest.'

'Oh, why's that?' she looked at me with some interest.

'I'm happy doing what I'm doing. I don't need it. I've only come because my agent sent me.'

It was true. I loved Winston's. I did little bits and pieces during the day, some television here, a day's filming there. I'd taken over from Jo Douglas, the regular presenter of *Six-Five Special*, the music show on TV and was also doing *The Jack Jackson Show*. Things were going really well for me.

So, feeling a bit cocky, I told this cleaning lady I was 'West End' and didn't want to go out to Stratford East, where the new musical would be.

'Aren't you a cute little thing!' she said. Cheeky cow, I thought!

Out on stage, Lionel Bart introduced me to his collaborator, Frank Norman, the writer.

'We're auditioning you for the part of Rosie, an Irish tart.'

'I can't do Irish to save me life.' This was untrue, but, as I said, I didn't want the part anyway.

Then a woman's voice came from the darkness at back of the theatre. 'Do you know anything about prostitutes?'

'Oh yes, I see all the Soho brasses on my way to cabaret.'

'Why don't you give us a Soho tart then? Show me what they do.'

This was irresistible. I started moving across the

stage. ''Allo mister, five bob for a wank, ten bob for an oral and a pound if you want the full card trick – it's cheap at a quid.'

I paraded up and down, pouting and wiggling my bum, completely over the top. I didn't give a monkey's. They all fell about. Then this lady said, 'Can you sing?'

'Oh yes, I'm a very good singer. Where's the pianist?'

'There isn't one. If you're such a good singer, you don't need a pianist.'

So I did my usual, *Sunny Side of the Street*.

'Thank you, I'd like you to be my Rosie.' Finally she came up on stage and I was face to face with the podgy woman in the woolly hat.

'Blimey, it's you – I thought you was the cleaner.'

'I know you did,' said Joan Littlewood, 'That's what I wanted you to think. You were behaving naturally, so I got you at your best. You got your job at the stage door.'

Funny the way you always land the jobs you don't really want.

Joan Littlewood and Gerry Raffles had already done much to put the Theatre Royal, Stratford East, on the map, with Brendan Behan's *The Quare Fellow* and *The Hostage*, and Shelagh Delaney's *A Taste of Honey*. Joan's unique and radical approach had really shaken up the theatre. Now the company were turning Frank Norman's play about Soho lowlife, *Fings Ain't Wot They Used T'Be* into a musical, with Lionel Bart doing the score. Miriam Karlin and James Booth would be the two leads.

Joan Littlewood took to me straight away, nicknaming me Birdsegg, because I was 'a funny little bird'.

On the first day of rehearsal, Joan said, 'This script's no good . . . we'll make it up as we go along.' I looked at her as if she'd gone bonkers. I was used to being told what to do. She had us all ad-libbing and generally playing silly buggers. I really thought she'd flipped her lid when she asked me to play Tosher, James Booth's part.

'I want you to go and find out what his problems are.'

Little did she realize I had problems of my own, namely that I couldn't take my eyes off James Booth. I ached all over for him. I'd taken a fancy to him on the set of the Jayne Mansfield film, *Too Hot to Handle*, but never plucked up the courage to speak to him. I couldn't believe my luck when I found I'd be working with him in *Fings*.

We went to the Stork Room one night after the show, with Albert Finney, who'd just made *Saturday Night and Sunday Morning*, and Jimmy got a bit jealous because Albert was making a fuss of me and dancing with me. That's when it started, Jimmy and me. He was heavily involved with someone else, so it never got really serious. Just a nice little ding-dong!

Two days before we opened Lionel Bart wrote a song for me called 'Where do little birds go?'.

'Just go and do it.' said Joan. 'Do what you want to do.'

Fings Ain't Wot They Used T'Be moved to the Garrick Theatre on 20 February 1960. I made my entrance with Toni Palmer who is five feet ten with legs up to her armpits. We looked comical even before we opened our mouths, a right pair of tarts. Boobs out front, bums wiggling behind . . . the audience loved it.

My number, 'Where Do Little Birds Go In Winter?', stopped the show. I didn't know what to do when the audience stood and cheered for more, so I said, 'I can't go on, Lionel hasn't written any more verses!'

Have you ever heard anything so daft?

Peter Charlesworth came round with the reviews the next day. He was in a state of shock. He said I'd hit the big time: 'Your life is going to change.'

The rave reviews were very welcome but the attentions of the Lord Chamberlain's office were not.

'Rosie must not sit with her legs apart in a pose indicative of copulation,' ruled the old buffer.

'What's copulation?' I piped up.

'Fucking, you silly cow,' said Joan. Well, I'd led a sheltered childhood, hadn't I?

To my surprise I became the toast of the town, playing to the rich and famous, then meeting them afterwards: Joan Collins, Anthony Newley, Warren Beatty, Bing Crosby – people I'd only ever read about in magazines or seen on the big screen. Had it not been for my regular visits to see Ronnie in Wandsworth prison, it would have gone straight to my head.

Despite what he'd said to me, I couldn't put Ronnie out of my mind. Mummy was livid when I said I wanted to keep in touch with him. The minute she'd learnt he was married and had 'undesirable connections' she moved heaven and earth to get him out of my life. She even went so far as to offer him all her life savings. But he wasn't having any. 'It's too late,' he told her, 'I love Babs and we're going to be married.' You can imagine how things had gone from bad to worse with Mummy after he was put in the nick.

I went to see Ronnie inside. He said, 'You're a big star

now, aren't you? You won't want to see me.' But I continued to go. I used to take him £2 per week out of my £28 wages.

Meanwhile, at twenty-three and better off than I'd ever been, I bought my first flat in Haringey. It was a relief to be away from Mummy.

I first met the Kray brothers backstage at the Garrick. They were ever so polite and gentlemanly. You could have knocked me down with a feather when Charlie Kray, the handsomest of the brothers – he was a dead ringer for Steve McQueen – invited me out for dinner. He treated me like a goddess, which isn't unusual for an East End guy; they know how to conduct themselves with women.

He took me with him to Eastbourne early one morning after we'd spent all night at the Astor Club in the West End. The porters at Eastbourne railway station were a bit taken aback to see this blonde number clip-clopping along in her mini-skirt and high-heeled boots. One of them came a cropper.

''Ere, Charlie.' I said, 'Look, that bloke's fallen off his barrer!'.

Although I was smitten with him at the time, my affair with Charlie wasn't a great passion and after six months together we cooled off and our dates sort of petered out. Then I found out he was married with a son he adored. Old Windsor had done it again. I used to take it for granted, when you went out with a fella, he wouldn't be married. I know, I know, green as a cabbage.

I heard later that Charlie went through a lot of heartache before deciding not to leave his family for me. He was the most gentlemanly man I'd ever met.

The business with Charlie helped me cope with missing Ronnie. He'd been moved to a prison in Kent, so my visits weren't so frequent now. But I continued to go. I'd write and continue to send him money to save. But I began to doubt if anything would come of our relationship. I didn't honestly expect him to leave his wife and family for me. In truth I didn't want to get married anyway. I just wanted to go out with lots of fellas and have a good time.

Miriam Karlin, my friend from *Fings*, had been signed up to do a TV comedy series called *The Rag Trade*, and when the producer, Dennis Main Wilson, came along to see our show, he said he'd like me to be in it, too. Miriam and I used to turn up at the TV studios on a Sunday, after a busy week in *Fings*, to record the show. I only had a little part in the first series, but it's amazing how quickly the public latches on to you. I had to start getting taxis instead of using the tube because of people staring or coming up to me.

I said I didn't want to do the second series of *The Rag Trade* because all I ever seemed to say was 'Shhh, girls, 'ere comes Mr Fenner!' When I complained about it to Dennis Main Wilson, he just said, 'You'll never make it as a comedienne, Barbara, you're far too pretty!' It was true that the leading English comediennes at that time were Irene Handl, Thora Hird, Hattie Jacques and Peggy Mount, and I couldn't help feeling things would have been different if I'd been American. However, for the next series, they offered me the part of Reg Varney's girlfriend, so I stayed.

Meanwhile *Fings* may have been the hot ticket in the West End, but Joan Littlewood always made sure we kept up to scratch. Instead of typing out discreet notes for each individual actor, she used to scrawl them in longhand and pin them on the noticeboard inside the stage door for all to see. The only person who never seemed to get a note was little me. 'What is it with you, you jammy cow?' said Yootha Joyce. Then one night I was in the middle of my big number, 'Where Do Little Birds Go?', for which I used to sit alone on the stage, when Toni Palmer and James Booth suddenly strolled on stage and started talking. 'That bloody perm, it's played havoc with my hair,' said Toni, just prattling away like that. I left the stage in a terrible state.

Toni said, 'I'm ever so sorry, Barbara, Joan told us to do it.'

'I'm sorry, Birdsegg,' said Joan when I confronted her. 'It's a terrible lesson, but you're singing it like Judy Garland, not a little Cockney tart. You look like you're in Carnegie Hall. You've been dying a death out there.'

She was right. The number was no longer stopping the show. As if that wasn't enough Windsor-bashing, I was then summoned to Miriam Karlin's dressing room and given another bollocking. 'Miss Windsor, you're misbehaving on stage,' said Miriam grandly. 'Just remember, you'll be a leading lady one day. You won't like it when you're out front and others start distracting the audience behind your back.'

Ronnie's sentence had been reduced to ten months for good conduct, and he'd been moved back to Wandsworth. Although I didn't want to marry him I still loved him and wanted him to feel good when he came out. So I bought new carpets and furniture for my flat in Haringey, hoping he'd want to stay with me, and I was there to collect him when he came out. We'd barely settled into a taxi when he asked me for some money – it turned out he'd sent most of the money I'd been giving him to his wife.

He said, 'I've got to stop off and see somebody.'

'I've saved another £35 for you,' I said, 'but I was going to give you a surprise.'

'But I've got to give this fella's wife a few quid.'

'But I saved the money for you,' I protested.

'Well then, I can do what I like with it, can't I? This geezer's in a terrible state. He has a wife and four kids and he's banged up inside. I've just got to do it. I'll get it back sometime.'

Ronnie and I started living together. I wanted to give him my all. But poor Ronnie had only been out of prison a few months when he was accused of being involved in an armed robbery at Lots Road Power Station, Fulham. We came home after midnight one evening and there was a loud bang on the door. I thought it was a neighbour in trouble. But I was wrong. It was the Old Bill, six of them on the doorstep.

They pulled the place apart, even took out the fire. Everything. On the table a newspaper carried the story of the robbery that morning. 'Reading about your exploits?' said one of the policemen. I screamed and shouted at them to leave us alone.

'Is she always like this?' another sneered.

I found a solicitor, Lincoln Ellis, who recommended a barrister to take on Ronnie's case. I was to meet her at Chelsea police station, where Ronnie was being held. What did I find but this girl who looked as if she was playing truant from school.

'She's too young,' I said, 'And she's too pretty!'

'She's red hot,' Lincoln Ellis assured me, 'one of my best.'

He was right. Nemone Lethbridge went on to make quite a name for herself.

I stood bail for Ronnie for the first time. It was £30. The press was out in force at the first hearing. There I was playing a brassy tart on stage and, behind the scenes, my boyfriend was being accused of armed robbery.

By the time Nemone Lethbridge had finished her investigations, the police evidence was in shreds. I listened to the verdict in the main hall of the Old Bailey. Of the eight men accused of armed robbery, Ronnie was the only one acquitted.

It was hard for Ronnie to get used to the idea of my being a celebrity after he came out. When we were out driving, we'd stop at traffic lights and people would start knocking on the car window.

All this made Ronnie very uncomfortable.

Appearances in public were very important to him. He said to me, 'Don't talk all the time.'

'Why not?'

'People will think we've only just met.'

I remember he always used to order the most expensive wine, because he didn't want to appear ignorant.

Ronnie got into fights if he overheard guys saying, 'Cor, I could give 'er one' or whatever. He'd say, 'Why don't you give me one instead!' He was brilliant with his fists.

We tried to live the same life as before, going back to all the old pubs. But there was an atmosphere. Someone would always resent us. One man got me to sign my autograph on a ten bob note then blew his nose on it. Ronnie knocked him out.

The huge success of *Fings* – it ran for two and a half years – enabled Joan Littlewood to go into production with a film about the East End, *Sparrows Can't Sing*, which she had been planning for years. The producers were more than happy with James Booth as the leading man, but they didn't want me in the female lead. They didn't think I was star material. Joan dug her heels in: 'Either Barbara gets the part or we don't make the film.'

Sparrows was made on location in Stepney in 1962. I suppose it did for the East End what *Room at the Top* had done for the North. I played Maggie, a young mum, whose sailor husband (James Booth) comes home to find she has moved in with a bus conductor (George Sewell), so he has to try and win her back. It was full of Cockney slang and fruity humour.

It was an amazing achievement for Joan, who had never made a film before. She used all the crowd from the Theatre Workshop, including Roy Kinnear, Murray Melvin, Avis Bunnage and Yootha Joyce, and we worked in more or less the same way – lots of ad-libbing and 'doing your own thing'. I think she found all the technical stuff rather traumatic. During my first close up the cameraman said, 'You're doing too much.'

'Fuck off,' said Joan. 'Don't tell my actress what to do!'

It was during the filming of *Sparrows Can't Sing* that I got to know the Kray twins better. We needed an East End club for some filming so I rang Charlie and they offered to make one of theirs, the Kentucky, available. They treated Joan like royalty when she turned up to see if it was suitable. God knows what the twins thought of her because they hated women swearing and Joan could never utter a sentence without a 'fuck' or two in it. Nevertheless Ronnie and Reggie were made consultants on the film, and they were around all the time when we shot the club scenes.

We needed some extras for the nightclub, so Daniel Farson, Joan's assistant, recruited some guys off a boat, about 20 of them, great burly buggers, all swearing like troopers when they arrived. Of course the twins didn't approve of this, so they took them all outside; I don't know what they said to them, but when they came back they were good as gold!

Princess Margaret was due to attend the première of *Sparrows Can't Sing* at the Rialto in Mile End Road, opposite the Kentucky, on 27 February 1963. Ronnie and I were driven there in a shiny Rolls-Royce and, as we approached the ABC, we could see that the Mile End Road was illuminated for the occasion, and lined with people waving. It was the East End's first royal première and the Krays, who had gone round knocking on everyone's door, intended making sure that the little local lady made good was given a real Cockney welcome. Afterwards we had a bit of a do at the town hall with the top stars in British showbiz, then on to the Kentucky, where we were served jellied eels, whelks, fish and chips, and other Cockney delicacies. The twins had the times of their lives.

3

By the time *Sparrows Can't Sing* opened to glowing reviews in February 1963, Ronnie and I had been living together for over a year. I was very much in love with him and, to my surprise, found I enjoyed playing the little housewife.

Ronnie isn't a very big man, though he somehow subtly gives the impression he is. Not really macho, quite soft-looking and quietly spoken. He had a sweet little look that endeared me to him. I used to love watching him in the bath. He used to wallow there every morning; he had a different bath oil and a different after-shave for every day of the week. Then I had to put Ronnie's rollers in for him, and blow dry his hair. He used to spend an hour on his barnet every morning – he was paranoid about having a hair out of place. While he was tweaking his hair I had to lay his clothes out for him; it had to be a different outfit everyday – suit or casuals – and everything had to match; shoes and suit, tie and shirt all had to be the same colour.

When I ran to catch the bus for rehearsals, he'd lean out of the window to wave me goodbye, and after the show he'd pick me up.

God knows what he did in between. Ronnie is very much his own man. Working for a guv'nor is alien to him. He is proud of only once ever having had a proper job – as a scaffolder.

He was born in Hoxton in 1933, at the height of the Depression. Hungry children had to roam the streets waiting for a chance to nick food or clothes. But Ronnie could always handle himself – it was the accepted thing for a row to be settled with your fists. He went to school with my mate Frankie Stephens, the cabbie, and the Kray twins, Ronnie and Reggie.

When I met him, Ronnie could barely read or write. At the age of ten he fell over and cut his leg badly. Tetanus injections were not freely available then and he contracted a poisonous infection. As a result he was off school for two years and had to wear a surgical boot. Still, there was no excuse for his illiteracy. His teacher said he had a good brain and he was wasting it. Being a rebel at heart, he simply refused to co-operate with any form of authority.

'Windsor, if only I'd listened to my teacher,' he used to say.

I tried to teach him to read and write, and also encouraged him to take singing lessons. He was always winning pub talent competitions singing songs like 'I could have danced all night' and 'Mother, I love you' in a high tenor.

But football was Ronnie's great passion. Despite his leg injury he ended up in Tottenham's youth team and the reserves. He could have gone on to play professional football, but then he married June, the prettiest girl in the school, when they were very young. He said June hated washing his muddy togs.

One of his friends said to me, 'If only he'd met you sooner, Ronnie would have made something of himself.'

Ronnie never had a lot of money in those days, but he didn't like being 'kept' by me. He had one ambition in life, to run a nightclub. But in the meantime, with no capital behind us, he was forced to try other ventures, like buying and selling toys. He set up a small factory to make oven gloves once, but it soon foundered.

I came home one day to find the kitchen table piled high with minced meat and jars of pills. The smell was awful.

'Come on Windsor, help me get this lot into meatballs and put vitamins in.'

'Balls? What for?'

'It's for the greyhounds.'

There we sat, like kids at the nursery, rolling out these little round balls of mince. The next night he came home in a rage.

'Those bloody pills, they're no good. The greyhound came last!'

'What do you mean, the greyhound came last?'

'I put pills in the meatballs and this guy promised to get them to the . . .'

'Hold on there, Ronnie Knight! Are you telling me you were trying to fix a dog? I don't believe it. I can just see the bleedin' headlines, FAMOUS ACTRESS IN DOG DOPE DRAMA!'

It wasn't until I made *Sparrows Can't Sing* that I realized Ronnie's connection with the Krays was more than tenuous. Ronnie had always been adamant that I shouldn't mix with them. He said he hardly knew them. But I began to hear stories about how Ronnie used to go around with the Krays, how once they had had an account to settle with a rival gang from south of the Thames, and they'd asked Ronnie to be their driver – Ronnie had an old black cab. It was very unusual to have a car at all in those days. They told him they had to 'sort someone out at the Royal, Tottenham'. It was simple. They'd go in, do the business, come out, and drive off.

Ronnie agreed to do it. When they got to the Royal though Reggie told my Ronnie they were short of a man and shoved a shotgun in his hands. 'Don't worry, we're not going to use 'em,' he said, 'just stand there and look menacing.' In the event he stood there white as a sheet and with his knees knocking.

All this was when they were in their early teens so I was a bit surprised when Ronnie got so hot under the collar about using one of the Krays' clubs in the film. To me the Krays were always charming and gentlemanly, typical East Enders. I take people as I find them. I don't pry or ask questions. I'd heard about things 'falling off the back of a lorry', I knew they made money from their clubs and that they had fingers in other pies but I didn't know whether any real villainy went on. I looked upon them as sort of Robin Hood figures, taking from the rich to give to the poor.

In their manor, Bethnal Green and the Mile End Road, there would be no muggings or street crime. The brothers were first in to help children, families and old folk who were down on their luck; there were always stories of their generosity to people in need.

Why should I regret my friendship with the Krays? They didn't walk around with knuckle-dusters looking for trouble. They only harmed the people who were out to harm them. You can only say what you feel about people and my feelings are that it's all wrong that they have been locked away for so long. I'll never change my mind about them.

I've kept in touch with the Krays over the years. Ronnie sent me some cuddly toys he made in prison, which I gave to charity, and I've been to visit Reggie. He often writes to me, very literate letters on all kinds of subjects. He gets up at 4 every morning and starts writing. I'm sure it's what keeps him going. He still looks immaculate. Considering the background of these men, it amazes me that they became so refined.

Similarly Ronnie Knight was refined in many ways. When I first met him, I had some vulgar ways I'd picked up in the clubs. In fact I dressed like an uptown tart. Playing Rosie in *Fings Ain't Wot They Used T'Be* was no effort! My agent, Peter Charlesworth, was the first to notice a change in me.

'I don't know who you're going with, but he's certainly good for you,' he said.

Ronnie felt he had every right to be possessive of his 'theatrical bird', as I became known to his friends. He had the East End attitude that if you've been going out for more than a month, chances are you'll be hitched within the year.

He never knew quite what to expect with me. 'It's never boring with Winsdor, she adds sparkle to my life,' he told a friend of ours.

He wasn't very happy when I went to America to promote *Sparrows Can't Sing*. After the British première the picture was sold and distributed in the US. It was the first time I'd ever been in an aeroplane – the first time I'd ever left the country, come to that. Peter Charlesworth came with me and we flew first class. We'd hardly parked our bums when they were dishing out the champagne and caviar. I said to Peter, 'Who's paying for all this? It ain't half going to set us back a few bob!'

'It's all free,' he replied.

'Get out of it!'

So I proceeded to knock back the bubbly like it was going out of style. Then I summoned a very prissy-looking BOAC stewardess.

''Ere, it's bleedin' 'ot in 'ere, open a few windows will you!'

When we got to New York, I made straight for Saks, the posh department store on Fifth Avenue, to buy a pair of gloves.

'Good morning ma'am, can I help you?' said a snooty assistant.

My head was scarcely visible above the counter, so Peter lifted me on to a stool. By now half the shop was eyeballing this close encounter of the Cockney kind.

'I wanna pair of gloves, darlin'.' I enjoyed being outrageous in those days. I tried some gloves on and said to the woman, 'They're very nice, darlin', but they're a bit tight across the wankatorials.'

'Tight across the wanka . . . what?'

Peter literally slid down the counter on to the floor, creased with laughter or embarrassment. I never did discover which.

When we got back from New York, there was a call from Oscar Lewenstein asking to see me for a film with Tony Hancock called *The Rhinoceros*. They wanted me to do a screen test, something entirely new to me. I said I didn't fancy that, but they asked me to come along anyway to meet Tony and have a chat. When Tony Hancock appeared, he suggested a bit of ad-libbing, 'Let's just bounce off each other!'

Afterwards he congratulated me. 'I've only ever seen you in *The Rag Trade*. I only knew you as a little bosomy blonde. I'd no idea you were so smart. Come and have a drink.'

We went to a pub in Shepherd's Bush. Vodka with tonic, vodka with lime, vodka with tomato juice, vodka with orange . . . he kept on changing the mixers. It was sad seeing him get drunk because he was a big hero of mine. We talked about being locked in our image. He hated the character he played in Hancock's Half Hour. He loathed the thing that had made him famous.

Next thing I heard, Tony was carted off to hospital to dry out, so the whole project had to be shelved.

Soon afterwards, Jacques Tati met Joan Littlewood in London and inquired about 'the little lady with the wonderful feet'. I was all ready to do a film with him but the Paris studios went up in flames. So that never happened either!

Even so, I'd been working my backside off since *Sparrows* came out – cabaret, recording, personal appearances – so I was glad to be heading off for the Cornish riviera in the summer of 1964 to do a film, *Crooks in Cloisters*, with Davy Kaye, Ronald Fraser, Wilfred Bramble and Bernard Cribbins. My role was a gangster's moll. Being almost the only female in the cast, they were forever playing jokes on me.

We were on the beach filming one afternoon when this really hunky young fisherman came in with his catch. He had a deep tan and beautiful blue eyes. Some of the cast decided to have a competition to see who would be the first to get him into bed. I started chatting him up and he invited me to go out on his boat. When I turned up, as arranged, at 4 the next morning, who should be waiting on the beach but Bernard Cribbins and one of the chippies off the set. They said they'd come along to chaperone me! When I took the young hunk back to my hotel room later, there was sand on the bed and an awful smell of fish: some of the others had bought a whole load of kippers and left them in my room!

Ronnie was always in the dumps when I went away on location. At heart he would have preferred me to give up the business altogether.

When June, who up to now had refused him a divorce, called to say she'd found someone else, he proposed marriage straight away. I think he thought it might make me give up my career, or at least stop me going away so much.

Funny thing was I became very nervous when Ronnie's divorce came through. When I couldn't get married I wanted to; when I could, I didn't want to. Contrary little bugger, I know. Ronnie said, 'If you don't marry me, I'm off.' I didn't want to lose him, so I said yes. With the divorce finalised in January 1964, we decided that March would be a good month to wed.

The whole thing still gave me the willies, though. Yes, we'd got on very well for the past three years, but I was putting my career on the line. Could I be married to a man like Ronnie and hold on to my place in the limelight?

I'm never nervous before a performance. But this was different. I sat anxiously in my canvas chair watching the hubbub around me. Stage hands were scurrying around with props and costumes while technicians wrestled with the heavy lighting equipment that looms over a film studio.

It was my first scene in my very first *Carry On*. Thank God for Bernard Cribbins! We'd got on well on *Crooks in Cloisters*. Now I felt like falling into his arms when I saw him on the set. 'Don't worry, they're a good lot,' said Cribbins. 'But keep an eye on Kenneth Williams. You never know what he's going to do next. He'll try to get you at it.'

I wish he hadn't told me because this first scene was with Kenneth. Talk about a fiasco! I messed up my lines, didn't I? You could have heard a pin drop, then Kenny took a deep breath. 'Ooo-h, da-ah-ling, do please get it right!'

His face was almost obscured behind a mass of black whiskers for his part as a British agent. It was all too much for me. I heard that he hated Fenella Fielding, so pulling myself up to my full 4 foot 10 inches, I retorted: ''Ere you, don't you yell at me with Fenella Fielding's minge hair stuck round your face. I won't bloody stand for it!'

There was a stunned silence as everyone waited for one of Kenny's sarcastic put-downs. Instead, he opened his eyes wide and clapped his hands, a grin spreading across his face:

'Ooo-h, isn't she marvellous!'

From that moment I was one of the gang, and Kenny and I became the greatest pals. The film was *Carry On Spying*, made in 1964, and eighth in the series that would make my name known the world over.

Ronnie and I bought a flat at Hendon Hall Court in north London, to move into after the wedding. Knowing my mother would be upset about it all, I decided to keep

*ove: Me at age two: my
*ther was pretty and
*ite . . . Daddy was a
*ical Jack-the-Lad East
*der.

*ht: Age nine, in
*dame Behenna's
*venile Jollities

Inset: *Johnny Brandon: my ve[r]*
first crus[h]

Opposite page: *My first glamo[r]*
pic at the age of eightee[n]

Left: *Age ten, with Dad at Scarborough*

Below: *In Aida Foster's 'Babes' at the Golders Green Hippodrome, age 14*

*With Jimmy Booth in 'Sparrows
Can't Sing'*

Above: At the premiere of 'Sparrows Can't Sing' with Ronnie

Right: On honeymoon with Kenneth Williams

Carry On . . .

everything to myself until nearer the date.

We wanted a private wedding. No fuss. No Press. On 2 March, the day before the wedding, the studio phoned to say they'd put me on standby for another day's shooting on *Carry on Spying* and would I stay by the phone until the afternoon of the following day! I told Ronnie we'd have to cancel the wedding, but he paid no attention. 'If we take the phone off the hook, we can be there and back within two hours,' he said.

I cried all the way to the register office. I kept saying I didn't want to get married. Ronnie stopped the car twice. To make matters worse, I'd lost so much weight, dieting for my film part, that my suit hung on me like a sack. I had to use safety pins to hold it together. We never made a *Carry On Wedding*, but we could have used mine for raw material.

When we were deciding where to go for our honeymoon, Kenneth Williams suggested Madeira. Glorious sunshine, avenues of palm trees, Kenny was making it sound irresistible. 'I know,' he clapped his hands together, 'We'll all go together!'

I was flabbergasted. Kenny pulled one of his faces. 'Well, you've been having it off with this chap forever ... you can hardly call it an'oneymoon.'

You couldn't argue with Kenny. He'd twist anyone round to his way of thinking. All the arrangements were made and on 28 March, with *Carry On Spying* in the can, Ronnie and I set off for Heathrow airport.

There waiting for us was Kenny, his mother Louisa, and his sister Pat. We found ourselves a seat in the cafeteria, thinking we'd have a nice little chat and a cuppa before Louisa and Pat waved us off. People kept coming over to me and Kenny for autographs, so much so that we missed our flight announcement. When Ronnie heard 'last passengers' over the tannoy, panic set in. Before I knew it, we were on the plane. I took a deep breath, prepared for take-off. It was only after lift-off, when I got up to go to the loo at the back, that I noticed some people I hadn't expected to see.

'Ronnie!' I grabbed his arm, 'What are they doin' 'ere?'

Sitting across the aisle were Kenny's mother and sister!

We were bound for Funchal, but our flight would only take us as far as Lisbon. We arrived in Lisbon all right, then suffered a two-hour delay.

'Oh my gawd.' I said to Kenny, 'What have you got us into?'

'Just look forward to the lovely ferry crossing,' he said.

But our troubles had barely started at this point. The next two hours were spent aboard a second aircraft which flew us to Porto Santo. It seemed like an eternity before we were ferried out in the dark to some anonymous object offshore – and meanwhile a terrible storm had been brewing. I was scared out of my wits when gigantic waves almost swallowed us all up as we climbed aboard the boat that would take us to Funchal. Even worse than the swirling seas was the nauseating stench on board, which set Kenny's famous nostrils flaring. The Bible stories of my convent days seemed to be coming to life before my eyes. Cattle, goats, pigs, chickens, chucked from side to side. People were throwing up even before the boat lifted anchor and there were no sick bags to be had for love nor money. Ronnie's face turned greener than Goodwood racecourse. He was throwing up so much, it was as much as I could do to stop him throwing himself overboard. 'I'm dying, I'm dying! Let me die!' he said. 'Let go!'

'Oh my darling, I love you! Don't leave me!' I said, hanging on to his legs the whole journey. The weirdest sight of all, though, was Kenny Williams making his way to the restaurant, hanging on for dear life. One lonely steward was in attendance.

'I've come for my meal,' said Kenny in his most authoritative voice.

'No one eats in serious conditions.'

'Well, I do.' He produced his sailing ticket. 'It says here that the ticket includes dinner and I want mine. I shall stay here till I get it!'

As if in a last rally before yielding to the ocean, Louisa's ghostly head appeared in the doorway: 'If my Kenny wants his dinner, he can 'ave it!'

In the early hours of the morning we docked at Funchal. We were all in a state of shock as we staggered off the boat. I don't remember who saw to the luggage, but we arrived at our hotel sometime after 3 am. Now the rain was coming down in torrents.

There didn't seem much else that could go wrong. Oh no? Our bridal suite consisted of one small room, no bathroom, no toilet. It was a right dump. Ronnie flopped down on the hard bed and groaned, 'Fuckin'ell! Prison was a palace compared to this.' Then he threw up.

I rushed down to reception. 'The room isn't big enough. My husband's a big fellow. His feet are hanging over the bed. Don't you understand, this is my honeymoon!'

Kenny heard me and stuck his oar in. 'I'll have you know I'm a very famous British broadcaster . . .'

That did it. Next day Ronnie and I were given a wonderful room, with a bathroom en suite.

Outside, the heavens kept up the onslaught. We thought the monsoon had arrived. Kenny gave up altogether. He hated everything to do with Funchal. 'I've come well equipped, Windsor,' he said, 'I've got these sleeping pills. They're the very latest. Made in France. They'll see me through this misery.'

I looked at the torpedo-like capsules he produced from his pocket. 'Bloody hell, they're a bit big, Ken, how on earth do you get them down your throat? Don't they get stuck?'

He said indignantly, 'You don't swallow them you silly cow, you shove them up your arse.' With that he flounced off to his room.

The vision of this indelicate and acrobatic operation made me laugh out loud every time I thought of it.

Kenny did put in an appearance from time to time with his dirty washing for Louisa or to chat with Ronnie. They adored each other. I used to pick Ronnie up on his grammar sometimes, and Kenny would tell me off: 'Let him talk how he likes.'

I spent most of the holiday in and out of the hairdresser. It was cold and raining, and there was nothing to do.

Most days one or other of the men went along to the travel agents to try and get us home. There was always some excuse – no boats because of the weather, no connecting flights. Tempers got a bit frayed from time to time.

Ten days later we were told we could begin the return journey. The following day the Famous Five flew to Lisbon where we stopped over. This was more like it.

A posh hotel and, more importantly, the sun was shining at last. For the first time since leaving London we relaxed.

On the last night Ronnie and Kenny and his mum went to a strip joint. A lady with big boobs did 'still life' poses while someone behind the scenes gave a commentary in Portuguese. Far from having the desired effect, all it did was give my boys the giggles. Some old blimp nearby took them to task. He said, 'Would you please show a bit of decorum. People like you make me feel ashamed to be English.'

'Shove off!' said Ronnie.

'It's none of your business,' said Kenny.

'It *is* my business. You're spoiling our evening and you're being rude to the young lady.'

'Don't you talk to my Kenny like that,' said his mum.

Ronnie stood up. 'Excuse me, sir, is there something about our behaviour that bothers you? If so, perhaps you'd like to come outside and tell me.'

It obviously did the trick – they spent the rest of the evening being plied with free drinks. They got back to the hotel pissed as newts.

Joan Littlewood phoned me just before I left for Madeira. Her production of *Oh, What a Lovely War* was so successful in the West End that she planned to take it to New York. Would I go with them? At first I refused because I'd been offered a part in a Peter Ustinov film with Shirley Maclaine. But Joan wouldn't leave it alone. Never one to mince her words, she told me what a boring actress I'd become: same old parts, same old characters. As usual, she got her wicked way – who wouldn't jump at the chance to play Broadway? I joined the cast of *Oh, What a Lovely War* for its last three weeks at the

Wyndham's in order to get used to it.

After a try-out run in Philadelphia, we came to New York and the famous West 44th Street – Broadway to you and me. Next door to us was *Golden Boy* with Sammy Davis Jr, opposite we had Carol Channing in *Hello Dolly!*; and down the road was Barbra Streisand in *Funny Girl*. Fancy a bunch of limeys like us pitching our tent among all these Hollywood sparklers! At least there was one reminder of home – Lionel Bart's *Oliver!* was still packing them in.

I'd left Ronnie on bad terms. I've always had a down to earth view of sex, and because I thought it wasn't fair leaving him on his own all this time, I'd said, 'I don't mind, you know, if you want a bit of the other.' He was furious. How can you be like that? What have I married?' he said.

'You're being paranoid!'

'Don't use those big words with me – you know I don't understand!'

I felt homesick almost directly I arrived. I said to our musical director, Shepard Coleman, 'I really hate New York. It's loud, overbearing and rude.'

Shepard burst out laughing – he laughed at almost everything I said. 'You'll feel better once we open,' he said. He was right, too.

On Broadway you soon know if you're a success. After the first night it's customary to go to Sardi's restaurant and wait for the early editions of the papers to come in. Word gets around pretty fast how the show's gone, and if it's gone down well, all the customers applaud when you walk in. If it's bombed, you walk in and nobody takes a blind bit of notice. It's kind of a ritual there. So we all turn up at Sardi's in our best bib and tucker, only to find they're not expecting us. Surely the reviews can't be that bad! Then the manager appears out of nowhere and waves his hand towards us in a grand theatrical gesture.

'Ladies and gentlemen, the cast of *Oh What a Lovely War!*'

They go bananas, everybody is on their feet applauding. I was completely overwhelmed. I remember getting to my table, Queen B. Once we were seated people started coming over. 'Oh we just thought the show was wonderful. You were just adorable . . . are you related to Her Majesty . . . have you been to Buck-ing-ham Palace?' You know the way they go on.

As the champagne flowed, Windsor's tongue loosened up. I became louder by the minute. 'Thank you, darlings, thank you, it was nothing, really!'

Fortunately we had a party to get to hosted by our producer, David Merrick. Slowly, I made my grand exit, giving the royal Windsor wave to all my lovely fans.

In the crowded entrance, the doorman hailed cabs for our party. I felt Peter Charlesworth nudge me.

'There's someone else who wants to meet you.'

'Oh, Peter, no more *dahling*, no more, we've got to get to that other do.'

'I think you'll want to meet this one.' Peter swivelled me round on my high heels. 'Barbara, this is Paul Newman.'

'Oh God!' I turned round and found myself staring into these amazing blue eyes, and I staggered backwards clutching my fanny – I thought I was going to pee myself. Then I partially recovered and behaved like any other spluttering fan. 'Oh, Paul, you're wonderful. I loved you in *Hud*, and what about *Someone Up There Likes Me* . . .

you were terrific in that . . .'

I even asked for his autograph on a napkin ('It's for my mum, Rose.') – how naff can you get? The poor guy never said a word. 'You were awful,' said Peter afterwards, confirming my worst fears.

After a while I was having such a good time in New York that I began asking myself why I'd married Ronnie at all. I didn't need it.

Victor Spinetti and I used to share a little table at Sardi's between the matinée and evening shows on Wednesdays. Victor who had rave reviews for his sergeant-major in *Lovely War* was great company, full of funny stories about people he'd worked with.

I caught up again with Johnny Brandon who came to see me after the show one night. Now a songwriter, he had settled in New York, and was as dapper and dandy as ever.

Then I fell for Shepard Coleman, our musical director, who'd won awards for *Hello Dolly!*, and was so elegant and distinguished-looking. Heaven knows what he saw in me! His wife, Gretchen Wyler, was six feet tall, sophisticated and a big Broadway star. He used to say to me, 'You do it all wrong, Barbara, but it's good what you do.' He loved to follow me down the street a few paces behind just to watch the reaction. The Yanks had never seen anything like it. He used to take me to smart parties with the New York intelligentsia. Shepard himself was so good to talk to, which, I had to face it, was a big relief after Ronnie. I began to realize then that even though the fucking had been so good with Ronnie, once, inevitably, lust began to fade, there was no meeting of minds to keep it going.

I was also asked out by a tough, Italian-stallion type

who came to see the show. He owned a chain of shoe shops and kept pointing out his name emblazoned across shopfronts when we walked down the street. He was charming and courteous, like my Ronnie – and it turned out he was Mafiosi! It must be my luck!

I came off stage once to find Warren Beatty standing in the wings. I took him off to the dressing room which I shared with Victor Spinetti.

'I must bring Lesley to see the show,' he said. Lesley Caron was the love of his life in those days. Sure enough, he brought her to see the show and, afterwards, when the four of us were having tea at Sardi's she said she was off to England shortly.

'Have a good time,' I said as they were leaving.

'Yes, Miss Windsor,' said Lesley, 'but remember, I have my spies!'

On the way back to the theatre, Victor Spinetti said, 'Warren's got the hots for you. I bet he gets in touch.'

'Don't be daft, Vic, course he won't.'

Warren phoned three times. But I found myself putting him off. I didn't want to be just another notch on his six-shooter. Recently I met him at the *Dick Tracy* première and he smothered me with kisses and said to my husband Stephen how he had been madly in love with me. The old smoothie!

Back home at the end of the run. I came to earth with a jolt. Ronnie was suspicious all the time, and badgering me about who I'd had it off with in New York.

Then I went to visit my grandparents in Stoke Newington. Nanny Ellis was very poorly in hospital, having fallen off a bus and cracked her skull. No one expected her to recover, least of all Grandad. He lost all interest in life and died soon after of a broken heart.

While I was mooching around Stoke Newington, a stranger came up to me: 'You're Barbara Windsor. I'm married to your father.'

I was gobsmacked! Julie was everything my mother wasn't – tall, slim and Jewish. She managed a card shop and Daddy helped out.

'I'm sure Johnny would like to hear from you,' she said.

I went there for dinner and he came over to my place. At first it was just like old times. He seemed genuinely pleased to see me and I thought we'd be able to get to know each other again. But somehow it all went wrong. Daddy and I wanted to turn the clock back, but you can't. People change and move on.

Peter Charlesworth got bad vibes about the new Lionel Bart/Joan Littlewood musical, *Twang*, from the start. Too many egos in one basket. He advised me not to do it. But after the success of *Oh What a Lovely War*, I wanted to star in a big musical again.

Rehearsals started in September 1965. James Booth was Robin Hood, and I was to play Delphinia, lady-in-waiting to Maid Marion. We were due to open in Manchester at the Palace Theatre before coming to London.

Oliver Messel, the distinguished designer, went to Paris and came back with this beautiful costume material that was so heavy you'd need weight training to dance in it. When Paddy Stone, the choreographer, pointed this out, Oliver snapped, 'You'll have to change your choreography!'

'No,' replied Paddy, 'you'll have to change your costumes!'

The writer, Harvey Orkin, who once worked for the

Marx Brothers, was confused by Joan's inclination to ad-lib. It wasn't so bad in *Fings*, where there was a cast of 12 and a handful of props. But with a cast of 60? She even told the chorus girls to do their own thing. Have you ever seen twelve chorus girls doing their own thing?

Give Joan a table, two chairs, a bottle and four people who've never acted in their lives and she'll give you a great little show. But give her a big budget, flashy sets and costumes, a top choreographer, and a famous Hollywood writer, and you're in for trouble.

Peter Charlesworth came up to Manchester to see the dress rehearsal. He found it incomprehensible from beginning to end. The dancers came skipping on in heavy, outsize costumes and then went arse-over-tit into each other.

At the first night of this long-awaited, star-studded show there wasn't a titter to be heard. Nothing. I had the least enviable line in the whole show: 'I don't know what's going on here!'

'Neither the bloody hell do we Bar,' came the reply, predictably. And 'It's not as good as *The Rag Trade*!' And 'Fings ain't what they used to be!'

James Booth was so fed up he refused to go out for the finale. 'Bollocks you are,' I said. 'We've done our best. It ain't our fault.' After *Fings* and *Sparrows*, two huge successes, neither of us could believe this was happening. Suddenly here we were with an audience baying for our blood. By the time we reached the end of the finale number, the theatre was empty. Next day there were queues at the box office – they were asking for their money back.

So much money had been invested in *Twang* that Bernard Delfont informed us they were calling in Burt Shevelove, the famous American director, to raise it from the dead. Burt was really positive from the start. He warned us it would be an uphill struggle, notes and rewrites every day, but he convinced us it was worth it.

Jimmy Booth resorted to putting all his rewrites on the back of the scenery. There was hardly a tree in Sherwood Forest that escaped his scribble. In one scene we had together, he couldn't find his lines because the tree he'd written them on had been taken off in a scenery reshuffle.

Few of us thought *Twang* would actually make it into the West End. *I* prayed it wouldn't. I was pregnant again. I told the management I wanted out. But they were still banking on Shevelove to pull a golden hare out of the hat. 'We're going to make it a hit. If you leave us now, darling, it'll die,' I was told. What could I do? I had a contract to fulfil. I went ahead and had an abortion.

Again we were barracked by the gallery on the first night. They seemed to have come along for the sport. Six weeks into the run, the notices went up. I'd aborted for the sake of my career again – and this time totally unnecessarily.

It may seem odd that I let things get to this stage, but in those pre-pill days people didn't know much about contraception. Ronnie thought it was demeaning to use a condom, then I had a coil fitted which went septic, so we tried the cap. The trouble was we didn't know how to fit it. Don't even try to imagine the contortions we got into trying to fit it in – me with my legs spread in the air, or Ronnie with his nose stuck up my arse. The trouble was that by the time we eventually managed it, the moment had always passed. Alternatively I'd take the time to fit it myself, thinking tonight's the night! – and then nothing happened.

4

Of the twenty-nine *Carry Ons*, I only did nine, yet I'm always remembered as the *Carry On* Girl. By the time I joined, the *Carry On* team – Kenneth Williams, Sid James, Charles Hawtrey, Kenneth Connor, Hattie Jacques and Joan Sims – were firm favourites with the British public. They were cartoon characters really, like the fat ladies and weedy men in the traditional seaside postcards. I was to become the busty floozy who tempts the weedy man away from his portly spouse. It was innocent titillation with emphasis on the tit!

My break came quite by chance. Ronald Fraser, who I'd met on *Crooks in Cloisters*, invited me to Pinewood Studios for lunch, while he was making a film called *The Beauty Jungle*. Pinewood's restaurant, I must tell you, is quite palatial, all wood panels and chandeliers. I'd arranged to meet Ronnie Fraser in the bar, which is at the far end of the restaurant. As I walked through the restaurant, I never guessed I was under surveillance by the producer and director of the *Carry On* series, Peter

Rogers and Gerald Thomas, who were looking for a bubbly blonde to replace Liz Fraser.

'Barbara isn't a sex symbol,' Peter Rogers said, 'she's a body, a bosom and a joke.' Thanks a lot, Peter. Anyway I got the job.

The *Carry On* scene everyone remembers is where I lost my bikini top in *Carry On Camping*. It was mid-November, freezing cold and pouring with rain. We were all ankle-deep in mud. Just to add to our misery, the special-effects people sprayed the mud green to make it look like summer time.

'I can't go on like this,' I told Gerald Thomas, 'Look at my feet. They're sinking!'

'I wouldn't be employing you if they were looking at your feet,' he replied.

I took my place in the line-up of girls representing the Chaste Place Finishing School for Young Ladies. We were doing keep-fit exercises under the supervision of our PT instructor, Kenneth Williams.

'Come along, Barbara, stretch out your arms, and fling, and in, and fling, and in, and . . . oooh!' My bikini top, unable to take the strain any longer, burst at the back, whizzed through the air and wrapped itself round Kenny's mush.

But, of course, in reality that didn't happen of its own accord. A fishing line was attached to my bikini top, while Bert, an elderly prop man, wielded the rod. You can just imagine them breaking the news to him: ''Ere Bert, we want you to take Barbara Windsor's bra off!' As the cameras rolled, Bert jerked the rod and started to reel in. My top didn't budge. 'Stop, Bert, stop!' I shouted, but he must have been hard of hearing because he kept on reeling in and I was dragged through the mud on my arse.

Covered from head to toe in mud, and freezing cold, I could hear Gerald rapping out his orders: 'Get 'er up and mop 'er down. Let's go for another take!' We had no choice but to get on with it.

When at last we'd got it right, I joined Kenny as we paddled our way back to our trailers. Kenny started winding me up:' It's a disgrace. It's an absolute disgrace!' I could contain my rage no longer: 'They treat you like a load of shit. We've never had a rise. I tell you, I'll never make another *Carry On* film!'

'Quite right, duckie' said Kenny.

Next day we saw the rushes. And, of course, they looked great. As the screen darkened and we got up to leave, I heard my voice loud and clear. I could feel my face changing colour. 'They treat you like a load of . . .' Everything I'd said the previous day was on tape! Kenny had forgotten to switch off the microphone round his neck – or that's what he said.

When I arrived for my next film Gerald said, 'Who's treating you like a load of shit then?'

When we'd started making *Carry On Camping* I'd tried to get away from my chirpy Cockney image. I played a rebellious pupil at the Chaste Place school for girls, and my opening scene took place in the shower room. I was meant to spy a peeping tom through a hole in the cubicle wall and squirt toothpaste into the hole, shouting 'Get away, you filthy snooper!' In the rehearsal I used a well-bred sort of voice, but things turned out differently when we came to shoot it. As soon as I saw this bulging eyeball ogling me I drew back and screamed 'Get aht of it, you dirty snooper' in my coarsest accent. From then on I was lumbered with the old Windsor rasp. I said to Kenny Williams, 'Oh blimey, I meant to play it posh!'

I always hated having to strip off. You'd never believe how quickly word got around when we were filming a saucy scene. One minute there was a handful of technicians, the next it was like a football match, with everyone jostling for position. It reached a point where I had to demand a closed set. 'Out you go, fellas,' I'd say. Nothing came undone until I was convinced only the director and the cameraman remained.

On one occasion when I'd finished my little strip, I happened to look up and there, perched in the rafters was a technician. He'd climbed up 50 feet just to get a bird's eye view of my boobs. I hope it was worth it!

When we were filming *Carry on Henry* I had to drop my dressing gown for a rear view shot, and I was making my usual big thing about clearing the set. Sid James had a go at Terry Scott for lingering. 'Come on, you, have some respect,' he said. As I came off, shaking from having had to flash my left buttock, I met a hairdresser from the neighbouring set, where Ken Russell was making *The Devils*. He said they were doing some pretty spicy stuff, orgies and the like, and he took me along to see what was going on. I peeped on to the set: it was full of technicians, cameramen, carpenters, a donkey and a monk having a wank under his cowl. And there was Vanessa Redgrave, stretched out on a slab, with the lights full on. Vanessa didn't bat an eyelid, and a moment later she was breezing past saying. 'I've got to fetch Jolyon from school'.

Stripping wasn't the only hazard facing me. I was Dick Turpin's sidekick in *Carry On Dick*, so I had to ride a horse. I was terrified of horses and I couldn't stand sitting astride them. I hated the feel of it between my legs. The director said, 'Can you ride?'

I said, 'Yes, let's do it. Don't let's rehearse, let's just do it!' You can still see the fear in my eyes.

In *Carry On Girls* I made the mistake of telling Gerald Thomas I could ride a motorbike. As I stood in all the black leather clobber, waiting for the director to shout 'Action!', Sid James asked me if I knew what I was doing.

'Course I do, it's like riding a bicycle, isn't it? You just get on and drive off.'

'Gawd, it's got gears and everything. You've got a lot of bottle, you have.'

It was a bit silly, I suppose, but I don't like people knowing I can't do something. I'd rather hurt myself than admit defeat.

I knew if I started thinking about it, I would have time to get nervous. I got on the bike, shoved it into gear and headed straight for a thick mattress Sid had had set up for me.

Another scene in *Carry On Girls* had me pushing one of my rivals for a beauty contest off a donkey and having a proper old wrestling match. At the end of the day's filming we'd only got half the shot, and the donkey had crapped everywhere. In the morning I said, 'You don't expect me to roll around in all that!'

'It's got to stay for continuity,' said Gerald.

'Sod the continuity!'

But, of course, it stayed.

The *Carry Ons* only had a six-week shooting schedule, so there was never any time to waste. It was a running joke at Pinewood that by the end of the first day's shooting we'd be an hour ahead of schedule and by the end of the first week, we'd be a whole week ahead. Gerald seldom allowed more than two takes. It wasn't Shakespeare; nobody analysed what they were doing, they just did it. We had to be there early, know the script backwards, cause no aggravations and endure all kinds of awful weather in order to finish on time. It was like going back to school.

The camaraderie among the team was great, though. I can picture them all sitting around on the set in between takes. Sid would be playing poker with the technicians, Charlie would sit by himself smoking his Woodbines, Hattie would do The *Times* crossword, and the others would gather round Kenny as he held court. 'Did you hear the one about the Canon with no balls?' he'd say. He'd tell the same stories over and over, but he'd always find a new way of telling it and making it hilarious again.

Then sometimes he'd try to embarrass me about my latest boyfriend: 'What's the size of his cock?' he'd say, or: 'Do you do *everything*? And then do you have to have it off with Ronnie when you get 'ome?' He was always teasing me. He used to say, 'Ooooh, Windsor, you smell so loveleee!' Once during filming he even claimed I gave him an erection: 'Oooh, she's given me the 'arf 'ard!' he said to the technicians.

As much as I loved Kenny Williams, I'd have to say Charles Hawtry was the best comic of the team. His timing was immaculate. It must have been all those years he spent making films with Will Hay. Like most of my *Carry On* mates, I met Charlie for the first time on *Carry On Spying*.

As spies, we were captured and held over a vat of boiling oil to make us divulge our identities. There were doubles and stand-ins on call, but Gerald preferred us to do our own stunts. It was a tricky scene to do, and when I'd unstrapped myself, I looked behind me to say something to Charlie.

'Gawd, he's fainted!' I yelled. We got him down and saw that his eyes were glazed and he was white as a sheet.

'Brandy, get him some brandy.'

'You're joking,' exclaimed Gerald. 'That's what's done it . . . the bleedin' brandy!'

I didn't know Charlie had a drink problem, did I? I soon learned, though. We came to know when he was pissed: he'd be very grand, arriving with his chauffeur carrying a crate of R White's lemonade. There were always one or two occasions on every film when he got really pie-eyed and would pass out. When that happened they would shoot round him. An hour or so later Charlie would come round and throw up. Once, I took over a bucket when he was throwing up in a corner – everyone else was ignoring it. But Charlie seemed to resent it. 'Oh why don't you piss off,' he said, 'you're always trying to be so kind and good to everyone.' It was so sad to see this wonderful comic actor, who I admired so much, ruining his life with booze.

Charlie had a hard time looking after his mother who suffered from senile dementia. He brought her to the studios every day and looked after her like a baby. He used to lock her in the dressing room when he was required on set. One day he forgot to turn the key and she got out. We were coming back from a take and we could hear this rasping voice echoing through the corridors. 'Have you seen my Charlie? I've got his tea ready and he hasn't come home from school yet!' We turned a corner and there was Charlie's old mum quizzing Sir John Gielgud.

Sadly Charlie misbehaved once too often, and, as a consequence, he was never used again.

We had some members of the public on the set during a scene in which Joan and Kenny were in bed together. I think they were quite shocked to hear Kenny passing wind rather loudly.

'How dare you!' exclaimed Joan. 'How do you expect an actress to work with you doing things like that!'

'I'll have you know Rudolph Valentino used to fart and *his* leading ladies never dared complain,' said Kenny.

Joan said, 'Yes, but they were silent movies.'

I'm sure the visitors thought it was all part of the script.

You didn't choose Kenny as a friend; he chose you. I felt very privileged to be numbered among his closest friends. He always used to say he liked me because I was the only one of the *Carry On* team who cleaned her teeth after lunch!

He had some funny ways. You couldn't phone him between nine and ten because that was when he was 'doing his ablutions' or cleaning the toilet; he was obsessed with his bowels. He had very few close friends and he could only deal with us one at a time. Stanley Baxter, who was a great friend of Kenny's, said he was sitting in a restaurant once when in walked Kenny with Maggie Smith. He took one look at Stanley and said, 'Come on, Maggie, we'll go somewhere else.' And he used to take against people for no reason. Joan Sims and he were great mates, but one day he said to me: 'Joan is so fucking suburban.'

So you never knew quite how to take him. He said to me, 'If you ever leave Ronnie, will you come and live with me?' Before I could open my mouth, he added,

'Mind you, there'd be no sex!'

My next stage show was a musical with Danny La Rue called *Come Spy With Me*. After it died initially in Oxford, we really worked on it for two weeks, and when we opened at the Whitehall, we began a successful run of eighteen months. Meanwhile Ronnie finally fulfilled a long-held dream – to own his own nightclub. He'd been working for a guy called Micky Regan, who owned a string of betting shops, and when the Artistes and Repertoire Club in Charing Cross Road came on the market, they decided to go into partnership. Ronnie was in his element at the club. He had such an easy, likeable way about him. He was a good listener and he knew how to treat people, make them feel welcome.

Though busy, I was feeling good about our relationship. Our weekends were a time for relaxation and routine. Ronnie came home early from the club on Saturday nights and cooked the supper, then I'd do my bit on Sunday, with the traditional roast we both loved.

I carried on our normal domestic routine at the same time as chasing around doing personal appearances and making TV programmes such as *Wild, Wild Women* and doing a stage show with Frankie Howerd called *The Wind in the Sassafrass Trees*.

I'd just returned from a brief trip to Canada, recording some old-time music hall programmes for television, when I received a call from Ned Sherrin asking if I'd be interested in doing a musical about Marie Lloyd, the great music hall star, to mark her centenary that year, 1970. I knew something about Marie Lloyd, because Grandad Ellis had often reminisced about her when I was little. I felt we had quite a lot in common – a couple of pint-size East Enders with bags of spunk!

The show, *Sing a Rude Song*, was a collaboration between Ned Sherrin, Caryl Brahms and Alan Bennett, and I had 31 songs to perform, including *My Old Man*, *The Boy I Love Is Up In The Gallery*, and *A Little Of What You Fancy*. Marie was a very emotional part. I had to sob buckets every night. There was singing and dancing and a punch up too. I had to age up to 50 during the show, which required loads of make-up and extra clothes. It was a heavy load for me to carry, and the show seldom finished when the curtain came down, because so many people who remembered seeing Marie in person wanted to share their experiences with me at the stage door afterwards.

My mother came to the first night and realized, perhaps for the first time, how much work goes into playing a part like Marie. But she had a funny way of showing her admiration – if that's what it was. In my dressing room afterwards, she said: 'Oh Babs, all that hard work. I wish I'd never taken you out of the convent!' My mother never made me feel she was proud of me. She loathed the *Carry Ons*. She said they made her see my Dad in me. She never wanted to hear about my affairs either. She said bitterly, 'You always get someone falling in love with you.'

Denis Quilley played Marie's first husband and Maurice Gibb of the Bee Gees the second. Maurice had never done theatre before, and he wasn't quite putting it across – he lacked grit or confidence or something. Ned said: 'I think you'd better give him one, Miss Windsor.' Anyway, no-one subsequently accused Maurice of not having any balls!

With wonderful reviews and sell-out houses, *Sing a*

Rude Song was a dead cert for a West End transfer, although we had to wait months for a theatre to become free. I consider *Sing a Rude Song* the best work I've ever done, but sadly during those few months *Oh Calcutta* opened. The whole tide of British theatre turned, and I don't think the show ever got the credit it deserved.

Shortly before we opened at the Garrick in May, I was struck by an even worse blow. Ronnie phoned from his club to say his younger brother, David, was in town and that he was taking him to a club called the Latin Quarter for a drink. 'Don't worry, we'll have a quick one then I'll come straight home,' he said. Just before midnight he called again, only this time he was in a terrible state: 'It's David – someone has killed him with a knife. What am I going to do, Bar?'

By all accounts there'd been a fight in the Soho club and David had been stabbed. Ronnie and his other brother, Johnny, went to the rescue too late.

I was as distraught as Ronnie. I didn't think I'd be able to go ahead with *Sing a Rude Song*. But you have to steel yourself when the alternative is letting so many people down.

As the months went by Ronnie couldn't get over his brother's murder. He was morose and always busy at the Artistes and Repertoire Club, which had become a popular haunt for BBC and music-industry people. On the rare occasions when we did bump into each other, I got the strong impression he didn't care any more. In fact I felt he'd married the wrong girl. He liked women with long dark hair and long legs – hardly what you'd call Windsor trademarks! I used to say to him, 'Who were you looking at when you asked me to marry you? It must have been someone over my shoulder.'

Even though I was starring in a successful West End show, Ronnie always had to come first. He expected me to lay his clothes out for him every morning – the usual suit one day, casuals the next. I got fed up running round after him. It wouldn't have been so bad if I'd felt appreciated, but he was never demonstrative. I felt I'd changed for him, but he never adapted himself in any way for me. He took me for granted. He never even said he loved me.

On top of all this, he was more madly jealous than ever of any man in my life other than him. He never missed an opportunity to snipe at Peter Charlesworth, my agent, who had guided me so well and been such a big influence on me as a person. 'You're not going to tell me you've never had if off,' he'd say. He'd go on and on. To be fair, I did talk about Peter a lot and we travelled everywhere together, and I suppose Ronnie felt excluded from our very close relationship. In the end, I dropped Peter because of Ronnie's pressure. It was probably the biggest mistake of my life. What Ronnie didn't realize, of course, was that losing Peter would make me feel even more insecure.

I needed someone to turn to, so I fell into the arms of John Reid. We met when I was doing *Sing a Rude Song*. He was only eighteen, very good-looking and flattered me rotten by saying he'd been to see *Come Spy With Me* umpteen times and knew all my numbers by heart. He swept me off my feet. He was a record plugger, just down from Scotland, and amazingly clued up about show business.

I fell madly in love with him. I loved the ambition and the drive. He said he wanted to go to America, drive a Rolls-Royce and become a millionaire all by the time he was twenty-one. Nevertheless, unlike Ronnie, he seemed genuinely concerned about me and my problems.

I made the mistake of introducing him to Kenny Williams, who said: 'I know all about you, because you know Stanley Baxter. You're wasting your time with 'er – she'll have it off with anyone. She sits there on the set eyeing them all up.'

'He's only joking!' I spluttered.

Later in the year, when I was doing pantomime in Norwich, John called in to see me. He was now working for Tamla Motown at EMI, and he'd just seen a new performer he was really excited about. 'I'm going to leave Tamla and give all my time to him,' he said, 'he's so good I just can't believe it. His name is Reg Dwight, but I've already decided to change it to Elton John.'

I first met Elton when he, returning unexpectedly from Paris, burst in on John and me in John's flat. John was cooking supper.

The next time I saw John he was driving down Baker Street in a white Roller, having just returned from America. 'I'm twenty-one next week,' he said as he drove off.

Our marriage was obviously in danger, so I promised Ronnie I would stop working for a while. But all that happened was I sat around feeling bored out of my skull, turning down offers of work, while Ronnie carried on exactly as normal. The only time he took me out was when I suggested it, and then it was to our usual haunts. I hated finding myself in this domestic rut. There were no surprises any more.

It was quite a relief to be able to return to work a few months later, especially as I was going to be working with Ken Russell on his film of *The Boyfriend*, Sandy Wilson's famous musical spoof, with Twiggy in her film debut.

I first heard Ken was planning the film while I was making *Carry On Henry* at Pinewood. The callboy told me I was wanted on the phone. 'Hello, this is Ken Russell's office. We're doing *The Boyfriend* and Mr Russell would like to talk to you about a part.'

The first thing I did was to look round for Kenneth Williams. When I couldn't see him, I knew he was up to his tricks again.

Next day at lunch, Ken Russell came over to my table: 'What happened to you last night? You were supposed to meet me at six o'clock after you'd finished filming.'

I could feel my face going bright red. It never occurred to me Ken Russell would want me to work for him. Ignoring my discomfort, he told me the part he had in mind for me was Hortense, a saucy French maid. Then he asked me to learn a song for the audition.

What audition! I was taken aback. It's not customary for established actors to audition, but when I arrived at the appointed place a couple of weeks later, I found everyone was in the same boat – Max Adrian, Bryan Pringle, Murray Melvin, Brian Murphy, each one dreading the ordeal of being put through their paces.

I finished my prepared song and dance with a few cartwheels. 'If you promise to do those in front of the camera,' said Russell, 'you're in!'

At the start of filming, Ken took each one of the principals out for dinner individually, presumably in order to find out what made us tick. He was very interested in life in the theatre, which is what his film was to be all about. When he asked me about making the *Carry Ons*, I told him that we never did more than a couple of 'takes' at the most on each scene because of the hectic schedules. I soon discovered that Ken can do as many as 50 takes before he is satisfied.

On my first day's shooting, he turned up wearing riding boots and carrying a whip, and said to the crew: 'Ladies and Gentlemen I'd like you to meet "Miss One-Take Windsor".'

'That's only when I have a director who knows what he's doing,' I replied.

The Boyfriend was demanding and traumatic. Filming took place at the Theatre Royal, Portsmouth, once a magnificent Victorian auditorium, which had since fallen on hard times. Now it was used only for boxing and wrestling matches. We had to put up with makeshift dressing rooms backstage, where the rain leaked through the roof and the mice saw no reason why they should vacate the premises for a bunch of actors.

Ken Russell lived up to his reputation as a hard taskmaster. It took 36 takes to do my big number, *It's So Much Nicer In Nice*. I kept to my promise and did the cartwheels, throwing myself all over the stage. I had to wear a big headdress with beads and my contortions were such that I actually managed to put my foot through it in what turned out to be the last take. Beads scattered everywhere as the whole thing fell apart.

'Yes, that's the take!' cried Ken.

'My beads have all broken.'

'That's what I wanted'

'If that's what you wanted I could've done it on the first take.'

'I didn't *know* I wanted it.'

So different from the *Carry Ons*!

Ken's quest for perfection got to everyone in the end. He even made us watch his old films in the evenings. We were all drinking too much and getting fraught. Poor Brian Murphy was so knackered, he boarded a train in Portsmouth to go back to London and literally went missing for two days. To this day I don't know what happened to him.

Ronnie visited the set once in four months and he chose the worst possible time to turn up. Ken was bored with making a sweet film by then and had decided to spice it up. While Twiggy had to look as if butter wouldn't melt in her mouth, the rest of us were made to go completely over the top. He'd already got one of the girls, Antonia Ellis, dressing up as a man and acting all butch. Now he had me doing a fantasy scene in which I had to perch up in a tree, like a Greek muse, wearing a dark wig. It was eight o'clock in the evening after a day's filming in the sweltering heat. Ronnie wasn't amused when I finally descended from my perch worn out, irritable, sweaty and covered in insect bites from head to toe. He never really understood the things we actors go through in order to keep our names in the limelight. I suppose he thought we were all barmy, and perhaps he's right!

Soon after that visit, Ronnie phoned to tell me he was going off to Acapulco with a couple of friends from the club. I couldn't believe it. We'd always gone on holidays together up till then.

After he'd gone, I got myself into a terrible state, what with the gruelling work schedule and hearing nothing from Ronnie for days on end – no phone call, no postcard, nothing. I began taking sleeping pills to help me get some much-needed rest.

One day during the filming, I was sitting in the dress circle feeling really down, when this fella leaned over me, and said, 'I like that number you did. I didn't know you did all that. I thought you only did *Carry On* films.' It was like looking at a young Paul Newman. We began talking.

One of the extras, Thomas Powell, was a lanky Portsmouth lad. His father, a hard man in the services, had always made him feel inadequate, so he'd run away to Paris, where he got hooked on heroin. Now he had kicked the habit and was trying to carve out a career as a guitarist and harmonica player. He invited me to go and hear him play. He was very talented, and I've always been attracted to musicians. I loved talking to Thomas. He used to teach me things. He got me to read *Lord of the Rings* and explained the lyrics of Bob Dylan, bringing me right up to date with what was happening intellectually and musically.

On the third day he found me sprawled on the bathroom floor of my hotel suite.

He said, 'Tell me to mind my own business, but do you take uppers?'

'What are they?'

'Do you take pills to get yourself together in the mornings?'

'Well, yeah, these black and white things.'

The pills I'd started taking had been having no effect, so I'd increased the dosage, and by now I was in such a state that I didn't know how many I was taking or when I was taking them. As an ex-addict Thomas recognized the signs.

I'd never thought myself capable of such a thing. I

could always cope, whatever the pressure. You read about celebrities taking accidental overdoses and you think, wait a minute, what's going on here? But it really was accidental in my case. I was unhappy and depressed, yes, but I never wanted to kill myself.

You can imagine how surprised I was to find myself in a hospital bed. Ken Russell was one of the first to visit me. 'What's wrong?' he asked.

'It's my husband. I think we're breaking up.'

I was detained for two days and when I came out, Ronnie called from Hendon: 'I'm just back from holiday. Where are you? Why aren't you here?'

'Don't bother to phone again, I've found someone else!'

It did the trick, because all these flowers started arriving at my hotel. Just as it seemed as though we'd reached the end of the line, Ronnie finally acted scared. He started bombarding me with presents and taking me out to fancy restaurants, giving me all the treatment, I'd always wanted; but it was all too late. The rot had already set in.

When I went up to do pantomime in Liverpool that year, it wasn't Ronnie who came up to see me, but Thomas Powell. It was Thomas, too, who escorted me to the opening night of *Jesus Christ, Superstar*, and the lavish party which followed it at producer Robert Stigwood's country estate. He let me down that evening by drinking too much and making silly accusations. John Reid saw that he was out of order and tried to calm him down, but the two of them got into a fight. There was blood everywhere, including all over Thomas's white suit. I should have seen then the way things would go with Thomas.

1972 proved to be a year of marked contrasts. At the same time as I was making *Carry On Abroad*, with all the gang, I was appearing in *The Threepenny Opera*, Brecht's version of *The Beggar's Opera*, with Vanessa Redgrave at the Prince of Wales Theatre.

I'd already played Lucy Lockett in *The Beggar's Opera* at Worthing, and the director Tony Richardson, Vanessa's husband, wanted me for the equivalent part, Lucy Brown, in the Brecht version. I had to be eight months pregnant, and I always began my entrance back in my dressing room, shouting and screeching about Macheath's treachery, reaching a crescendo as I stormed onto the stage.

Macheath had betrayed me, Lucy Lockett (4ft 10½ins) with Polly Peachum, played by Vanessa, who was already on stage, all 5ft 10ins of her. Then we went into this duet together, and we often used to get the giggles. I used to say, 'We mustn't laugh. I'll get the sack.'

'What about me?'

'No, It's all right for you, because the director's giving you one!'

Arthur Mullard was also in the show and in the pub afterwards Big V, as I called her, used to get Arthur and I to sing all the old Cockney songs.

Being back in London, I was living at home with Ronnie again. I decided I ought to try to forget Thomas. But one night we were sitting watching Paul Newman in *Cat On a Hot Tin Roof*, and, because he reminded me of Thomas, I got up and telephoned him. I thought: he's the big love of my life. I promised I'd leave Ronnie. As a result he moved up from Portsmouth to London, and got a job in a bar. I even went out and put a deposit down on a flat for Thomas and me.

But Thomas was quickly becoming desperate. 'When are you going to tell Ronnie?' he kept asking. He began to get drunk all the time and make scenes. He lost his job.

I couldn't help remembering what Ronnie had always said: 'You'll never be anything without me. You'll end up in the gutter. When you met me, you were a naughty little lady with too many boyfriends who drank too much.'

Then one day when Thomas and I were having a row, he took all his clothes off in the middle of Shaftesbury Avenue. 'You've always hidden me away,' he cried. 'Now let everyone see me.' I began to worry my life was spinning out of control.

5

In all my *Carry On* years they'd never provided chauffeur-driven cars to get us around. We were always expected to arrange and pay for our own transport. That is, until *Carry On Girls* in spring, 1973, when they suddenly decided to send a car to take Sid James and me to Brighton for three days' filming. It seemed odd, especially as the rest of the cast were going by train.

The car picked me up first and then we drove to Sid's house near Pinewood Studios. Waiting to greet us at the end of a very long drive was Sid himself. I didn't know him very well at the time, so it didn't make sense and I was a bit suspicious about what could be going on.

On the drive to Brighton he asked me about the stage show Peter Rogers wanted to do with the *Carry On* team. I told him I wasn't interested in doing it, but Sid persisted: 'You're the one we want. We need the glamorous type. We need someone who can sing and dance.'

It was about five o'clock in the afternoon. I was just settling into my hotel room when the phone rang. It was

Sid, inviting me to his room for a glass of champagne. His balcony doors were open and there was a bottle of bubbly on ice and uncorked. He brought up the subject of the stage show again.

'Is it the money?'

'God no.' I said. 'It's just that the theatre is very special to me. I choose my work very carefully.'

Then his wife phoned and Sid put his finger to his mouth. 'Shhhh, it's my wife!' he said as if to warn me to be quiet. I was taken aback. It wasn't as if we were up to anything in the first place! As I made to leave, he said: 'There's half a bottle of champagne left. I'll put a spoon in it to keep it fresh. Will you come back and finish it with me?' I said I would, but I never did.

When we'd done our bit of filming in Brighton, it was back to Pinewood. Sid was ever the gentleman, opening doors for me and paying me lots of attention. I wasn't enjoying *Carry On Girls* because all the 'bathing beauties' were lovely, leggy 18-year-olds. Sid noticed how nervous I was. 'What's up with you, little lady?'

'I can't cope with this,' I told him. 'All these lovely young things.'

'How can you say that? Look at all that personality shining through – they don't have that. You should see yourself in the rushes – you're fabulous.'

Sid kept the pressure on for me to do *Carry On London*, as the stage show would be called. 'If you're not going to do it, that's it then,' he said one day, with a dramatic flourish.

'What do you mean, that's it?'

'Without you, we can't do it. It will have to be called off.'

You had to hand it to Sid – he was a crafty old bugger.

He knew I'd cave in once I thought my reluctance to do the show was putting everyone else out of a job. There was also my ego to consider – few *Carry On* fans knew that I was first and foremost a song-and-dance lady, and *Carry On London* would be the ideal opportunity to set the record straight.

I seldom saw Ronnie during filming – he came home later and later every night. We only seemed to see each other at the weekends.

Thomas's behaviour, too, was becoming increasingly erratic. Late one evening the police rang to say he'd been in a terrible fight at the club where he was a D.J. Someone had slashed his face with a knife. He thought he was dying, and asked a policeman to phone through a message: 'Tell her I love her.' Thank God Ronnie wasn't in, or Thomas's life really would have been in danger!

Carry On London previewed in Birmingham. It was a disaster. We members of the Carry On team were like compères introducing a series of variety acts. After the dress rehearsal I suddenly took over. The way I fought to get a number into my Cleopatra sketch prompted Sid to nickname me 'Tiger'. He always came to the side of the stage to watch me doing my routines. He'd never seen me assert myself like that, nor had he ever seen me in front of a live audience.

'I didn't know you could do all that!' he said with a look of astonishment.

One night while I was waiting to go on for my Cleopatra routine, Sid whispered in my ear, 'I dreamt about you last night.'

'Did you?'

'No, you wouldn't let me.'

It was like a *Carry On* gag, but Sid didn't laugh.

Sid's dresser had failed to turn up, so Thomas volunteered to stand in for him. My lover was helping my would-be lover get dressed!

While we were still in Birmingham I went out with a few of the cast for dinner. Jack Douglas ordered a seafood concoction and, like a fool, I ate it, knowing damn well the effect it would have. After dinner I returned to the hotel. The minute I opened my door I threw up. At that moment Sid phoned and asked me what I was doing. I told him I was getting ready for bed. He asked if he could come down, adding, 'Will you make my dream come true?'

'Sid, you won't believe this but I've just been sick. I'm sorry, darling, can I take a rain check?' It was putting off the evil moment.

The next morning he was waiting at the bottom of the stairs and walked me to rehearsals. 'I'm ever so sorry about last night,' he said.

'There's no need to apologise, Sid. It's a compliment. I'm flattered that you fancy me.'

Sid told me it wasn't just sex. He said he liked my sense of fun, my funny mixture of doziness and outrageousness. But I thought: he just wants to give me one – wallop! – and that would be it!

Carry On London opened at the Victoria Palace on 4 October 1973. Thomas had been good to me throughout this tour, and on *The Owl and the Pussycat* tour. Now he said: 'I must come to the opening night. I'm always with you.'

'You can't come. Ronnie will be there. You've got to promise.' Later, at a reception at the Embassy Club, he tried to bluff his way in, despite being roaring drunk. He proceeded to threaten the doorman and behave appallingly. When he turned up the next day at my hairdresser's and said, 'Come on, let's go out for a drink.' I told him straight that I didn't want to see him again.

'I know I behaved dreadfully,' he said. 'What can I do to make it up to you?'

'I'm sorry, Thomas, we're finished. I've got to get myself back with Ronnie.'

It had been at the back of my mind to sort my marriage out. Things had reached a point where Ronnie and I had to either decide to make it work or split up completely. As I was leaving the theatre the following night, Thomas barged into my dressing room in a drunken stupor again.

'I said I didn't want to see you . . .'

'Can I wash myself?' he asked.

He filled the basin with water. Next thing I knew there was blood all over the place. He had cut his wrists with a razor. Then he plunged his head under the water as if he were trying to drown himself. I grabbed his long hair and tried to wrench him away from the basin. I don't think he really meant to kill himself, but he certainly succeeded in frightening me. I put a makeshift bandage on his wrists and pushed him out of the door, where we ran straight into Bernard Bresslaw on his way home. Bernie could sense something was wrong.

'Are you OK?'

'It's fine, Bernie, we just had a little accident,' I said, trying to make light of it. When we got outside I called a taxi and took Thomas straight off to hospital. I was furious with him for putting me through this, and I just wanted to be rid of him.

Carry On London was a happy show, nevertheless.

Peter Rogers, our producer, came to see us all every Friday, viewing the show from the royal box in typically grand style. Afterwards he would come round with a crate of champagne. The fans waited in coachloads at the stage door for autographs.

Hardly a day went by without a bouquet of flowers from Sid. I never did anything to encourage him, but working in such close proximity meant I couldn't avoid him. He always left his dressing room door ajar so he'd be able to see me passing. He'd always call me in. I couldn't keep saying 'No', could I?

I kept telling him I had to go home every night. However, when some of the cast were asked to do Pete Murray's radio programme, *Open House*, live from Victoria Palace, Sid saw his chance. As those taking part were asked to be at the broadcast by 8.30 in the morning, overnight accommodation was laid on. Sid asked if he could take me out to dinner the night before we went on air.

'Oh no, darling, I've got to go home and get my beauty sleep, especially as I'll have to get up early the next morning.'

'Aren't you staying at the Royal Lancaster like the rest of us?'

'I only live ten miles away. I've always gone home. I can't tell my old man I've got a broadcast and I'll have to stay up in town.'

Then Tony Wells, our press agent, started on about me staying in town with the others.

'Actually Barbara,' he confided, 'I know what all this is about. Sid's got the hots for you and he thinks this is his moment!'

I was in a quandary and I knew there was no way Sid

would let me off the hook. He kept up the pressure for the whole intervening two weeks. I felt well and truly cornered. Eventually I told Tony Wells I would stay at the Royal Lancaster – for the good of the show!

On the night of my dinner date with Sid, I wore a white fox-fur hat to match my coat. When I got to his room, John Inman was sitting there with his partner, Barry Howard.

'Isn't she the most gorgeous thing you've ever seen?' said Sid.

After dinner we went back to the Royal Lancaster and he disappeared to his room and I to mine. He told me he'd come back later. I was in such a state. I just wanted to get it over with. It'll get all the passion out of him, get it out of his system, I told myself. Don't get me wrong, I liked Sid, but I never fancied him – he was thirty years older than me.

An hour passed and nothing happened. I was almost asleep when the phone went in my room.

'I'm sorry to keep you waiting, Babs. I had to wait for Val to phone me back.'

When he came to my room, he kept saying, 'I love you'.

I ordered a couple of drinks to be sent up. When the waiter arrived I said, 'They're both for me you know!' Then I flung them both down me throat.

'I don't know what you expect,' I said. 'I'm not a fiery little sex symbol. I'm nothing like that sexy image.' God, what am I going to do? I thought. I couldn't get out of it. I was worried, too, because at that time, as was the fashion, I wore several hairpieces. I thought, Christ, Sid's going to run his hand through my hair and at the height of his passion it's all going to come off!

He said: 'I'm too old for you. I wish you'd seen me years ago.'

Let's just say the earth didn't move that night.

In the morning I really squirmed when, after the previous night's misadventures, Pete Murray introduced me as 'Britain's very own sex symbol'.

I was wearing a crochet dress and while I was parading up and down on stage at the Victoria Palace, someone in the audience yelled, 'You've got no drawers on!'

I was wearing all-in-one tights but the lights were so strong it looked as if I had nothing on underneath. It wasn't long before a pair of drawers appeared on stage. Rather than go off stage, I put them on over my dress. When I looked towards the corner of the stage there was Sid laughing his head off.

Once the show got into a twice-nightly routine I soon forgot my embarrassment with Sid and we became the best of mates. Believing the episode had blown over, I was stunned two weeks later when, standing there dressed up as a woman – in my Cleopatra outfit – he said, 'Barbara, I'm really madly in love with you.'

'You're joking, Sid. You're not in love with me!'

'Yes, I am. We've got to go to bed again!'

I just stared at him. I was struck dumb.

He said, 'I love you and you don't care, do you?'

I found my voice at last: 'I love you, Sid, but as my leading man. You're fabulous as Sid James. But what happened between us, it was nothing.'

'Nothing! You were even more wonderful than I could ever have imagined.'

Did he really mean these things, or was he acting a part?

As the weeks went by I simply drifted into an affair with Sid for the sake of a quiet life. But Sid's passion began to affect the whole cast and crew as well. By now everyone was talking about him behind his back. He continued to stand in the wings whenever I was on stage, but now if anyone so much as whispered when I was on, they'd be for it.

'This has to stop,' I told him. 'You're putting me off.'

Some time later I was coming off stage and Sid staggered past me gasping for breath. I thought he was ill, but the stage manager said it was due to climbing all those stairs.

'What stairs? His dressing room is on the ground floor.'

The stage manager explained how Sid had started running up to the top of the theatre at every performance so he could watch me from a box at the back of the balcony. I knew about Sid's heart trouble. There was no way I wanted to put undue strain on his heart, so I told him to go back to watching me in the wings.

Unfortunately Sid did not stop at watching. He was now jealous of me talking to anyone, and even stopped me going to the pub across the road.

He was furious when I got Thomas Powell a job at the Victoria Palace. Once again Thomas had attempted to take his own life, this time with an overdose of sleeping pills. I realized then that Thomas was basically a nice guy but he couldn't cope with life. When we'd met I had been at my most vulnerable. I needed love and affection, and I had plenty to give in return. Ronnie had been giving me none. So I had focussed my love on Thomas. Now I felt responsible for him.

Because of the scar on his face and damage to his

nerves, he was unable to play the harmonica the way he used to. I decided to pay for him to have plastic surgery. He looked and felt much better when he came out.

But it wasn't long before Thomas heard all the gossip about me and Sid: 'It's not true about you and Sid James is it? It can't be!' I suppose it was silly of me to put them under the same roof. They became very bitter. What was worse was that it was not unusual for Thomas to come to work pissed, and in that state, his behaviour was entirely unpredictable.

One night he threatened to drop something on top of me on stage from the 'flies' where he was working. When I came out to do my Cleopatra sketch, I was terrified. How I remembered my lines or even what I was supposed to do, I don't know. My mind was elsewhere. I kept looking up at the lights and dodging from one spot to another going to the opposite of every position I was meant to be in. The rest of the *Carry On* gang thought I'd gone stark, staring bonkers. They would be talking to me one moment, then I'd disappear behind them the next. Even our little dance routine began to look like an Apache war dance as their eyes followed mine up to the rafters. It wasn't so much exasperation in their eyes as confusion and concern. They knew something was up.

Sid, not surprisingly, was the first to grab me when I came off stage. 'What the hell's got into you, Tiger? Have you gone completely off your rocker?'

I felt I had to tell him, both for my own and Thomas Powell's safety. He was in no fit condition to be working high up above the stage. When I finished telling Sid, he went straight to the box office, borrowed £100 and paid Thomas off. I was heartbroken. I didn't want him to go, but I was in an impossible situation, keeping three men going. I was terribly wrong in the way I behaved, stringing Thomas along. If I look back at it now, I should have kept Sid at arm's length and left Ronnie. It was Thomas I really loved.

Before the end of the run, he came back to see me, this time with a girlfriend by his side. He looked more relaxed and together than I'd ever seen him. I heard later that he'd married the girl and settled in New Zealand. I was pleased for him, and happy that we'd parted friends.

Carry On London was not without its fair share of drama. I was on stage singing 'You Made Me Love You' on Boxing Day when the theatre was shaken by an enormous bang. Some members of the audience, clearly confused and worried, stood up and started muttering, so I said, 'I don't know, some people will do anything to get me off the stage!' I went to the front of the stage and told the orchestra to keep playing, then I turned to the audience: 'You wouldn't leave a little Cockney girl up here all on her own, would you? C'mon everybody, let's sing along . . .'

Even the people standing up, who seemed to be rooted to the spot, started joining in. Even so, we didn't manage to drown the commotion going on outside. It was like the Blitz all over again.

As soon as the fire curtain came down, the house manager stepped forward to announce that a bomb had gone off next door in a pub called the Stage Door. As everyone suspected, the IRA had carried out their threat to extend their bombing campaign to London. He urged everyone to stay seated; the show would go on.

Sid rushed up to me when I came off at half time. 'Are you all right, Tiger?'

'Course I am, darling; you're forgetting I was a war

baby.'

When I got to my dressing room, all the windows were smashed in. There was glass all over the place and my two dogs were howling. Dorothy, my elderly dresser, was sitting down, her head in her hands, in a state of total shock. But a decision had been taken to continue the show, and I had a costume change to make.

When *Carry On Dick* started filming in February 1974, I was seeing Sid almost every hour of the day. The strain of our relationship was beginning to tell – on me at least. In one scene I had to seduce him. While I was being half-hearted about it, Sid was playing it for real. Our director, Gerald Thomas, who knew nothing of our liaison, thought Sid was misbehaving and gave him a good ticking off. The trouble was that with Thomas Powell out of the way, Sid seriously considered he had the field to himself. He seemed to forget I was married.

At the finale of *Carry On London* the gang paraded along the catwalk, singing 'Smile' and waving goodbye to the audience. Bernard Bresslaw helped me back on to the stage.

'You know, Barbara,' he said, 'we've done this show for over six months now, twice nightly, and this is the first time I've ever helped you off the catwalk. I feel dreadful I haven't done it before!'

'That's all right, duckie,' I said, and left it at that.

As we walked to the car on our way home, Bernie turned to me: 'Can you believe it, Sid said I mustn't help you back on stage again? He doesn't want me touching you.'

You can imagine how furious I was. It was also annoying me that Sid was no longer covering up our flirtation. Intimate notes which should have been put not just in an envelope but a thick seal, too, were pushed under my door on bits of paper or left around for anyone to read. One day the wardrobe lady apologised to me: 'I'm sorry, Barbara, I shouldn't have read this, should I?'

At parties he'd always sidle over to me and start talking intimately even when Ronnie was around. One night when Ronnie and I arrived at a big showbiz function at the London Hilton, Sid was outside pacing up and down by a public call box. He said he'd been trying to call us because he was worried we'd had an accident. We were only half an hour late.

Once inside and seated, Sid threw another tantrum because he wasn't sitting next to me. As soon as someone moved from the table, he took their place and so on until he was sitting opposite me! Worst of all, when the actor Jack Hedley made a cheeky remark, Sid took umbrage on my behalf.

'Look,' said Ronnie, trying to calm him down, 'don't get yourself into a fight over my missus.'

Upset as I was over Sid's ridiculous antics, I was still concerned for him. The poor man was frantic over me and it began to show in his general health and demeanour. Ever conscious of his heart trouble, I thought it would be best if I left *Carry On London*. I told Peter Rogers I would leave after six months when my contract expired. When Sid heard he burst into tears.

'If you leave, I'll go as well,' he said. This was no idle threat, and Sid's leaving would have a more catastrophic effect on the show than mine. When Peter offered me more money I found myself giving in once more, not because of the money, but to save the show.

I was so unhappy. I wanted desperately to leave, to

have some time to sort out the mess my personal life had become. In the event, fate took a hand and made the decision for me.

For a newspaper publicity stunt, I was asked to dress up as Britannia. It was part of the *Daily Express* 'Get Britain Back To Work' campaign during the power workers' strike. Weighed down with shield, helmet, buckle and Union Jack I could scarcely move. Not surprisingly I tripped and damaged my back. I didn't take much notice at first, but after the exertions of two evening performances I found my body had literally seized up. I had a terrible struggle even to get out of the car. Then I found I couldn't climb the stairs to our maisonette, so I had to sit at the foot of the stairs until Ronnie came home.

My doctor said the only cure was complete rest. My understudy, the buxom Anita Kaye (who later married Jess Yates) took over in *Carry On London*.

The irony of it all was that Ronnie really turned up trumps. His genuine concern made me feel all the more guilty about the Sid business. When it became obvious I was making little progress, he carried me down to the car and we did the round of the osteopaths. He even took me to a faith healer. But it was a specialist who got to the root of the trouble, which, as I'd already suspected, was more to do with stress than anything physical.

When I finally returned to the show after three weeks, Sid and producer Peter Rogers had bought a whole barrow-load of flowers from the florist outside the theatre and put them right across the stage. I was really touched by that.

In April 1974 Sid bought an apartment in the South of France. While his wife Val went off to set up home, he looked for a flat in London. He found what he wanted in Dolphin Square, an exclusive block of flats in Pimlico, not too far from the theatre. He said it was to save him commuting every day from Iver.

Although it was written into our contracts that we should have two weeks' holiday a year, Sid only took one. He spent it in Marbella, staying at the luxury Don Pepe hotel on its outskirts. He phoned me from Jimmy Tarbuck's place nearby, saying how much he missed me, how he longed to get back.

Sid's wife was spending a lot of time abroad now. By this time I suspect she'd begun to realize something was going on between us. Perhaps she hoped that we'd see the error of our ways if we were left together over any length of time. In many ways I wish she *had* stayed so that it wouldn't have been so easy for Sid and me to carry on. I was making regular visits to the flat in Dolphin Square and I began to think I was in love with him. Sid was so kind to me; he made me feel good. He told me he had ten good years left and that he'd like to spend them with me. Sex with Ronnie was pretty well over by now. Sid was highly sexed and very explicit about what he wanted to do. But he was also very romantic, and used to get the pianist to play some slushy love song like 'The First Time Ever I Saw Your Face' whenever we walked into our favourite restaurant together.

I wanted to please him, too. I enrolled in a Cordon Bleu cookery course because I knew Val was a great cook and Sid was used to high standards. I only lasted one lesson and Sid thought the whole thing was hilarious. I was very nervous the first time I cooked for him at Dolphin Square. Well, the only thing I actually cooked was jacket potatoes, all the rest was cold meats and smoked salmon. It was never eaten anyway because he got a phonecall saying his house in Iver had been burgled, so he dashed off into the night.

As *Carry On London* neared the end of its run, Sid became more masterful about our affair. 'Right,' he said, 'you're going to leave Ronnie and I'll set you up in a place in town. I'll go to a hundred quid a week.' My first reaction was to do exactly as he said. I found myself a mews house near the Royal Albert Hall. He told me that I must tell Ronnie I was leaving him, and he would tell Val the same.

As I say, Sid was giving me all the attention and affection I missed in my relationship with Ronnie. I really felt we could be happy together. So, that weekend, I started to get my house in order. Ronnie couldn't understand what I was up to. He knew Sid had a thing about me, but never saw any reason to take it seriously. When Sid phoned on a Sunday, Ronnie used to say, 'Why does he bother to call you on his one day off? If he wasn't so old, I'd think there was something going on!'

It was proof, if proof were needed, of how far Ronnie and I had grown apart. I made up my mind to leave him forever.

6

That weekend Ronnie's father died suddenly and, though saddened by the news, I also felt relieved. I now had an excuse for delaying leaving him. 'We'll give him time to get over his loss,' said Sid.

Then as I was leaving the Victoria Palace one night with Sid, one of the stagehands said somebody wanted me on the phone, a reporter from the *Sun* newspaper.

'What do you feel about Zomparelli being killed?' asked the voice on the other end of the line.

'Zefferelli? I don't know, I never worked with him.' I didn't know what he was on about.

'No, not Zefferelli, Zomparelli, the man who killed your brother-in-law.'

Sid could see I was confused and took the phone from me. He confirmed the man in question was Zomparelli. My heart sank. Zomparelli had been gaoled for four years for murdering Ronnie's brother David and released a few months earlier than expected. On 4 September 1974, he was gunned down in the Golden

Goose Arcade, Soho, not far from where David died.

Ronnie knew that if anything happened to the man, he and his brother Johnny would be prime suspects. He even joked about employing a bodyguard to look after him. At first the Old Bill believed Zomparelli had fallen foul of a gang involved in the amusement arcade business, then they ran true to form and came for Ronnie. But because of lack of evidence, they had to let him go almost as soon as they'd arrested him.

I had to tell Sid that I couldn't leave Ronnie while all this was going on. It was a terrible blow for him. What made it worse was the fact that he wouldn't see me regularly any more. *Carry On London* was due to finish a month later.

Sid slid downhill rapidly, turning an awful yellow colour. It worried me tremendously. I thought it was his heart, so I decided to tell him straight, 'It's no use, Sid. I don't feel I'm good for you. In future I'm going to come to the theatre, do the show and go straight home.'

'But why? Why are you doing this to me?'

'Because I know you're not well . . . and you won't even have a check-up.'

Next morning at eight o'clock my phone rang. It was a man saying he was Sid James's doctor.

'Mr James has had a very honest chat with me. He is suffering from complete exhaustion. His heart is fine. Unless he's going to throw you round the room, or swing on a chandelier, he'll be perfectly all right.'

Then Sid came on the phone. 'Are you satisfied now?'

Despite this doctor's reassurance, I knew he was far from well. The discs in his back had started giving him trouble, which made him walk strangely, and we had to go through everything in the show to see how we could make it easier for him. I suggested we cut out a sketch where he had to pick me up and run off stage with me over his shoulder.

'No, darling, you're as light as a feather. We mustn't cut that!'

It sounds daft, but Sid couldn't bear to lose anything in which he came into physical contact with me.

A week before the show closed, Sid was in a terrible state: 'I can't go on, I can't work! I've been advised to go away and lie in the sun. I've told Val I don't want her coming with me.'

'But she should go,' I told him, 'She'd look after you.'

He was adamant and confused at the same time. He couldn't face the last night, which was unlike him. I felt concerned about Sid's illness and his absence from the show, but what could I do? He went off to Spain to stay with his agent, Mike Sullivan.

Ronnie and I went back to his sister's villa in *Benalmadena*. It was obvious to me that Ronnie wanted us to have our own place out there, so when we saw a site for sale near his sister's, with panoramic views of the Spanish coastline, we snapped it up straight away. All we needed now was some money to build a villa! It was Ronnie's idea to pool our resources with his brother, Johnny. Later we would plant some trees and grass. We were going to call the villa Casa Rocca, because it was in the shadow of a rock, until we realized every toilet in Spain bore the trade name *Rocca*! In the end we christened it Villa Limonar instead, very refreshing, after some lemon trees we bought and planted.

On my return from Spain, I started rehearsals on a

series for ATV Elstree called *Carry On Laughing*. I didn't really want to do it, having just done such a long run in *Carry On London*, but Sid started turning the screws again, and promised me he'd hassle them for more money.

I wanted just a working relationship with him. He gave me his word, but soon he started making unfair demands of me.

I said: 'Look Sidney, you're making me ill! The way you keep phoning me, demanding to know what I'm doing, following me, checking up on me. It's got to stop!' I might have saved my breath. He wasn't taking it in. In the end I got very angry – Sid, unlike Ronnie or Thomas, could never reduce me to tears. I decided to phone Gerald Thomas and say I couldn't do the series. 'I don't think it'll work with Sid the way he is,' I told him. Gerald was very understanding.

'If you feel you must go then, you must,' he said, 'but, Barbara, there is only one person to put an end to the whole business with Sid and that's you.'

When the scripts came through, though, they were wonderful. They allowed me to play several different parts. So I decided to change my mind on one condition. I was not due at Elstree for three days after rehearsals started, so I called Sid and said unless we could be working mates and nothing more I wouldn't do the series. He assured me it would be as I wanted and everything would be okay. But the minute I arrived at Elstree I knew I'd made a mistake.

'A round of applause for our beautiful Miss Windsor,' he exclaimed when he saw me. 'Isn't she lovely!' he said to anyone who'd listen.

At lunch it was customary for the *Carry On* gang to

eat together, but Sid insisted we ate on our own. Afterwards I ran into my old mate Danny La Rue.

'I can't believe what I'm hearing about you and Sid James. How could you?'

I told him how I'd become involved. 'I'm in a Catch 22 situation . . . I can't get out of it.'

During the rehearsal period, I received an invitation to make a presentation at the *Evening News* film awards. Evidently, when Sid heard about it he obtained tickets, though he tried to convince me later he'd also been invited. You could have cut the atmosphere with a knife. Here was my leading man sitting a few feet away and I couldn't even talk to him! I can't say I was surprised when Val turned away and completely ignored me. They never should have come in the first place. There was a message for me backstage. It read: 'I'm sorry. I love you. Don't get upset.'

Next day I tackled him about it: 'Please tell Val it's over. We'll do this series, then after that it's got to stop. You'll be in Australia. We'll stay good mates, but that's it. When you come back, you'll have forgotten all about me.'

We got through the series but it wasn't easy. He clinged to his idea of leaving Val and getting a place for us somewhere. At Christmas he bought me a magnificent diamond. It was set in jet surrounded by heart-shaped smaller diamonds. I said, 'I'm sorry, Sid, I can't accept it. It's far too personal and far too expensive.' I gave it back to him, but it arrived by special delivery the next day.

Sid was due to leave for Australia on 28 December 1974. He begged me to meet him at the Dorchester before he left. I arrived at 11 o'clock, wearing a leopard-skin coat with a matching trilby hat. Sid looked dreadful. He could hardly stand. He said, 'I love you Barbara, I'm going to Australia to do this job and when I come back I'm going to sort it all out.'

I didn't put up a fight. I just thought, once he gets away, that's it. *Finito*! Then he said, 'If we're not going to get together, I can assure you I shall be dead within a year.'

'That's nice darlin'! Here I am having tea at the Dorchester in me posh hat and you're telling me you're going to pop off!'

I thought if I could make him laugh all the time, I could keep him at a distance. It did relieve the tension for a moment, but then he said, 'I feel trapped'.

I knew he meant he couldn't cut himself off from Val.

I said, 'My marriage has gone from bad to worse because of you. I wouldn't be at all surprised if Ronnie found someone else. And I wouldn't blame him.'

Then Sid asked me about the one-woman show I was taking to New Zealand, *Carry On Barbara*. When I told him there were four boys in the show with me, he demanded to know who they were.

'There's two gays and two straights. I'm going to have a right old time with the boys!'

I was only trying to raise a smile again because he looked so miserable, but Sid hated me talking dirty. I decided not to mention the six musicians who were going too!

He put me in a car and said to the chauffeur: 'This is the most wonderful girl in the world. I'm so much in love with her, but she won't have me.'

The next day Sid left for Australia. I still had a lot of work to do on my show.

I arrived in Auckland, New Zealand, in early

February 1975. Two days before we were due to open, the producer came to my dressing room, carrying a crate of champagne. 'I saw Sid James last week. He sent you this . . . and a note to go with it!' He laughed in a nudge-nudge, wink-wink sort of way, and handed me a piece of paper folded in half, no envelope. Sid had written 'To the most wonderful lady in the world. Wishing you all the success you deserve. I love you. I'm waiting for the day we can be together.'

I was livid with Sid. I knew the producer had read it. How could he embarrass me like this?

The success of *Carry On Barbara* helped me put the Sid business to the back of my mind. It was marvellous travelling everywhere by coach, seeing all the geographical wonders of both the north and south islands of New Zealand. But when we arrived at a place called Wanganui in glorious mountain country, there was a message waiting for me at the hotel. Sid had called. 'How the hell did you track me down?' I demanded. He said he had my itinerary for the tour.

'I suppose you've forgotten all about me now,' he said. 'You've found someone else, haven't you?'

It was the same old stuff on both sides, him saying how much he missed me, loved me, wanted us to be together, me saying, 'Yes Sid, no Sid.'

He rang off abruptly when Val came into the room. After this phone call, I resolved to finish it once and for all. Calmly and confidently, I sat down with some hotel notepaper and started to write: 'The main reason I'm writing this letter is to say you are making me desperately unhappy. I don't want to live with you. I don't want to be with you. I would far rather you got out of my life.'

It was a very 'together' sort of letter. Pages and pages about our relationship. I didn't spare him anything, and I didn't hear from him again.

After I returned from New Zealand, towards the end of April 1975, I did an eight-week tour of England with the show, now renamed *A Merry Whiff of Windsor* and produced by Cameron Mackintosh. In September and October of the same year, we took the show to South Africa, under its original name. I hadn't seen Sid since the day after Boxing Day, 1974. On my last night in Johannesburg, the *News of the World* phoned from London asking about Sid James. As I was about to go on stage, there wasn't time to talk to them.

Ronnie seemed cold and distant when he met me at the airport next day. Then he showed me the paper. It hinted at an affair with Sid James.

'Tell me it's not true?' Ronnie demanded.

'Come on, Ron, don't be a silly bugger.' I felt this was the one time I could say it without feeling guilty.

In November 1975 I started rehearsals for *Aladdin* at Richmond with Jack Douglas, Jon Pertwee and Una Stubbs.

During a break one day Jack said, 'Guess who I saw when I was coming out of my house and getting into my car? Sid James. He wants you to phone him.' He gave me Sid's rehearsal room phone number. Jack Douglas lived next door to Thames Television, where Sid had just started a new series of *Bless This House*, his popular comedy show.

Jack also said Sid was planning to take the comedy play *The Mating Season* on a tour of Britain.

'He'll be so miserable,' I told Jack. 'He hates the theatre, he hates farce and he hates touring!'

The only reason Sid ever toured in anything was to see the world. He wouldn't just fly to Australia for a tour and come straight home. He always stopped off somewhere, like Singapore or Hong Kong or even Las Vegas, for the gambling. He liked going to South Africa, too, because that was where he was brought up. But touring round the UK in the middle of winter sounded like utter madness for him. I thought of phoning him to try and stop him, but I worried I would start things up again.

Before *Aladdin* ended its sell-out run at Richmond, I had a visit from Keith Michell, then director of the Chichester Festival Theatre, asking if I would consider playing Maria in his production of *Twelfth Night* later that year. My first reaction was 'I can't do Shakespeare', but I had to admit I'd always secretly wanted to have a go, so after a bit of persuasion I said 'Yes'.

Another slice of good fortune that came my way was a series of TV commercials for the Milk Marketing Board at Shepperton Studios.

On the way, my driver said Sid James was also doing some filming there. At first my heart sank, then I felt that, after such a long separation, I could cope with seeing him again.

All morning I wallowed in a bath of milk while the producers of the commercial bickered over how they wanted me to play it. The buyer wanted me slinky and seductive, like Bardot, the producer wanted me playful and flirtatious, like Monroe. It didn't bother me as I was having a lovely time while they topped up the tub with buckets full of milk. My skin had never felt so good! There was one little problem. The sheer volume of milk made my boobs float on top. Hard as they tried to get them to stay down, nothing worked. In the end I had to wear a body strap.

By lunchtime they were no nearer deciding how it should be done when a waitress came over to our table.

'Hello, Barbara, good to see you here,' she said as if I were a long lost friend. Needless to say, I'd never met her before.

'That's it!' cried the director, 'We need someone the public can identify with. Like the waitress, everyone feels they know you. Barbara, just be yourself!'

After we'd finished shooting, I was escorted back to my dressing room. 'Could we ask you not to come out until we tell you?' said the floor manager. I thought it was an odd request but I agreed, thinking I'd have plenty to do in the dressing room. Outside I heard a familiar voice. It was Sid James with his wife, Val. I could vaguely hear them arguing.

'You're not to see her,' I heard Val say.

'I'll do what I want!'

'Don't be silly. I've told you. I don't want you to see her again.'

I knew they were talking about me. Much as I wanted to chip in, I kept quiet till they'd gone. Then, disregarding my orders, I went along to make-up.

'What's going on here?' I asked the make-up girl.

'We had this message that on no account were you and Sid James to come into contact with one another.'

When I won the 'Bottom of the Year' Award for 1976, the press seemed amazed that I'd been picked to play Maria in *Twelfth Night* at Chichester. It was to be staged from May to July. In April I went with the rest of the cast, including Gordon Jackson and Michelle Dotrice, to a press reception at the Chichester Festival

Theatre. I came back by train to Victoria and jumped in a cab. As we were passing Victoria Palace, the cabbie asked me if I still saw the old gang.

'How's all the gang? How's your old Sid James?' he said.

'Oh, he's smashing, lovely.'

The phone was ringing when I opened the front door.

'Is that Miss Windsor? This is the *Daily Express*. I'm sorry to phone you with bad news.'

'What news? What's it about?'

'It's about Sid James.' Then he paused. 'He died earlier this evening.'

He told me Sid had died at 7.30 on stage at the Sunderland Empire. He had come out on stage, started a scene, then suddenly slumped to the floor where he remained. They brought the curtain down and called for a doctor. But he was already dead. I've never cried so much in my life. When he came in, Ronnie said 'I hope you'll cry this much for me when I die.'

I couldn't go to bed. They gave me days off rehearsal. I just sat in my front room. He'd died and we weren't friends. All these 'if onlys' kept spinning round my head. Inevitably they were all guilty ones. If only I'd called him to persuade him not to go on tour. If only I'd brazened it out with Val at Shepperton. Then I remembered his words to me at the Dorchester when he'd said he would be dead within a year.

Sid had been a great mate. I wish he was around today. Despite all the traumas we had a really good time together.

I was offered one other *Carry On* after Sid died. *Carry*

On Emmanuelle would feature Jack Douglas, Peter Butterworth and Kenneth Connor, each dreaming of their ideal woman. I was to appear in various stages of undress to suit each guy's fantasy.

The script really hit rock bottom. It was everything the team would not ordinarily do – more like one of the *Confession* films. I knew Sid would not have approved of it, and neither did I. Hardly had I turned the part down than a newspaper called to ask if it was true that I'd walked out on *Carry On Emmanuelle*. 'I've never been on the set, let alone walked off it,' I said.

Next morning the papers were full of me walking out of the studio, describing the film as 'soft porn' and 'one long nude scene'.

I put it down to the publicity boys. You get used to it in my business. Even when you deny things, a lot of people still believe what they've read. As it turned out, I made the right choice. *Carry On Emmanuelle* proved to be a disaster, both with the critics and the public.

I never got over Sid's death, but work is the best way to overcome grief, and I was glad to have my big challenge at Chichester in the months ahead. At first I found the language very difficult, as I'd only ever done modern dialogue, and the director, Keith Michell, seemed to think I could manage on my own. But I was helped a great deal by Bill Fraser, playing Sir Toby Belch, whom I knew and admired as a comedy actor. He said one day in a rehearsal, 'Don't do it as if it's Shakespeare, just say the lines as if you were doing a *Carry On*', and after that I was okay.

Ronnie and I were invited to appear on Derek Batey's programme, *Mr & Mrs*. Because of his shyness, Ronnie didn't want to do it, but his mother and I managed to persuade him it would be fun. After all the cracks about him being a villain, I wanted viewers to see what he was really like.

Amazingly, we got all six questions right, and Ronnie proved a hit, receiving lots of fan mail afterwards. It went so well we were invited back for a festive special, coming on as Mr & Mrs Christmas Knight. Again Derek remarked how well 'tuned in' we were to each other. Little did he know!

In the autumn of 1977 Ronnie and I decided to buy a house for the first time ever in our married lives, thinking it might bring with it a change of heart. Also my mother had been going on about how we could afford a house 'after all those years at the top'.

We moved from Hendon to Stanmore. Mummy thought Stanmore was too far away. Now it was: 'I suppose you'll use that as an excuse not to visit me in Rayleigh!' As I say, I could never win.

Soon after, she and Len decided to sell up and live nearer me. I found them a nice flat at Bushey, just down the road from us. She and Len were a great help with the big house she'd talked me into buying. Len had retired from his carpentry business and I think he welcomed an opportunity to keep busy. Being with Mummy 24 hours a day, he now realized I wasn't to blame for every quarrel when we'd all lived together. 'You never know how she's going to be, do you?' he said to me. 'She's got some funny ways!'

One day, we'd just come indoors, when I found Len doubled up with pain. He said it was probably indigestion. Mummy thought it might be an ulcer.

I arranged for him to see a specialist and he was sent for tests. When we all went to visit him in hospital, his whole family was there, too. It seemed as if we all had a premonition.

All his tests proved negative. The surgeons decided on an exploratory operation. I asked him if he was nervous. 'I can't wait to wake up and find it's all gone,' he said. 'If you knew the pain I was in . . .'

The exploratory revealed inoperable cancer. They could do nothing for him. It was a tragedy Len had to die in such pain, unable to enjoy his retirement. All he wanted was to do the things with Mummy that he had been unable to do while he was working. He was the sweetest of men.

Our move to Stanmore had not brought about the change in our relationship I'd hoped for. Ronnie was as kind and generous as he'd always been, but deep down it was still wrong. When we moved in the neighbours said we'd bought a white elephant. The house had a history of tragedy. Hardly had we settled in than my poodle, Freddie, took ill and died. Then during the panto season at Bradford, I tripped on stage, said 'Hello everybody! My name's Aladdin!' and fell over and broke my arm. The audience split their sides, thinking it was intentional, but all I wanted to do was cry.

Another sad blow for me was the death of Beryl Fordham, a dear friend since the mid 1960s. She was a wealthy Jewess, one of the most beautiful women I've ever seen. She was also everything Ronnie disliked in a woman – bossy, independent and outspoken. The feeling was mutual: she could never understand why I'd married a guy like Ronnie. She used to say to me, 'It's do this and do that. How on earth do you put up with it all the time?' The odd thing was she was very similar to Ronnie in many ways; her whole life was concerned with what she was going to wear that evening or the next day. As with Ronnie, everything had to be done to accommodate her.

She had had cancer before I met her. She was always saying that she and John Wayne had kicked the big C. When she was suddenly taken ill again, Ronnie and I went to see her. It was the day before she died. As we drove home, Ronnie began to cry. 'That pretty little lady . . . why does she have to go?'

Once again work helped me to carry on. Despite my injury, Bradford proved enjoyable. When the season ended, Danny La Rue got in touch to ask if I'd like to do a TV version of *Come Spy With Me*. As it was 12 years since we appeared together on stage, I thought I would be too old for the part. Danny disagreed. Even my broken wrist didn't deter him. I had to remove the plaster for the filming, so it was a painful few weeks.

I took a break after that and went with Ronnie to Spain, but the trip didn't end our run of misfortune. We had now built our Villa Limonar into the side of the majestic Sierra Nevada. It was a typical whitewashed Andalusian holiday home, with a sun terrace, patio and swimming pool. There was still a lot to do inside. So I suggested to Ronnie that we took a trip to nearby Fuengirola where there was a lovely furniture shop.

Soon after we'd entered the shop there was an almighty crash. I can't describe the shock effect. We looked up and saw a massive petrol tanker crashing through the plate-glass window in an explosion of glass. I panicked and started to run out of the front of the shop.

'No!' Ronnie yelled at me, 'I can smell petrol!'

He grabbed me and pulled me towards a side door. I tried to pull away, but he literally flung me through the door. Then he jumped over the broken glass and got the salesman out as well. He was amazing. The moment he was free, the whole place erupted into a fireball. The fire was following us along the pavement where the petrol had been spilled. Then we heard kids screaming and babies crying.

'I've got to help the babies,' Ronnie shouted.

'No, you'll be killed! I'll never see you again!'

As he headed back to the shop, I grabbed his legs, and he dragged me along with him. I wasn't going to let go. There was nothing he could do.

We learned later what had happened: a little girl had run out into the road and caused the driver of the tanker to swerve to avoid her. Because it had been raining, he skidded and went out of control.

Nine people had been killed instantly. Two bodies were found in the shop. Had it not been for Ronnie's swift and selfless action, both the salesman and myself would have been added to that list. I told Mummy what had happened and she wrote him a touching letter thanking him for saving her daughter's life.

Ronnie and I spent the rest of our holiday in a state of shock.

After Len died, we added a granny flat for my mother to the house in Stanmore. We also bought a baby grand piano for the lounge, which opened out on to a verandah and lovely gardens. I like doing interior design, working out colour schemes and choosing furnishings and carpets. In the beginning with me at home all the time Ronnie loved the new house. From the moment he got out of bed in the morning, the ritual began. First the singing, then a bath, followed by the morning paper. Then he'd go and sit in his favourite antique armchair in the lounge. 'This is all mine,' he'd say, casting his eyes around the room. Mummy and I would laugh our heads off.

But he seemed to love the villa in Spain even more, and he often stayed there for weeks at a time. Mummy was company for me then, as was Kenny Gibson, Sid James's dresser, who came in to help me round the house. We enjoyed talking about old times.

I got a phone call in the summer of 1980 asking me to do a week's filming in Brixton on the children's series *Worzel Gummidge*. I accepted. Then the day before filming was due to begin I heard that a car was being sent to pick me up and take me to my hotel. A hotel in Brixton? Then it became clear. It wasn't the London suburb at all, but Brixham in Devon, the pretty harbour town. When I told Ronnie I'd mixed up the locations, he accused me of lying and refused to see me off.

Once I arrived in Devon my first thought was to phone him in the hope he'd be over it. But there was no phone in my room, and the pay-phone in the lobby was out of order. When I got through eventually, he repeated his silly accusations. He said he couldn't believe there wasn't a phone in my room. I suppose he thought I was doing all this to stop him checking up on me.

Filming began on Monday. I was the figurehead on the ship, *Saucy Nancy* (actually a replica of the *Golden Hinde*, anchored in Brixham harbour). Saucy Nancy falls in love with Worzel and competes with Aunt Sally, played by Una Stubbs, for his affections. This meant leaving the prow from time to time to pursue him.

Because ship's figureheads don't have legs, I was strapped to a little trolley on runners. The final scene saw me returning to the ship at great speed before my absence was noticed. For this, little railway tracks were laid down the high street of King's Somborne, a nearby picturesque village. When the stunt girl heard that the trolley would hurtle along at 30 miles an hour down this hill she got cold feet. So it was me that the crew strapped to the trolley and started pushing.

The first couple of times nothing happened – the trolley refused to move. At the third attempt it did, but in the process I was badly gashed high up in the groin. I was in agony and by the time I got to my room there was blood everywhere. I didn't tell anyone, but I suffered internal damage which still causes problems to this day. These stunts can be really dangerous when not done by professionals. I could so easily have been killed. Look what happened to poor Roy Kinnear. But you can't think of that at the time. You just get on and do what you're told.

I felt sorry for myself on the journey home and looked forward to some sympathy from Ronnie. But I was forgetting it was Friday, one of his nights out with the boys. I went straight to bed instead.

If I'd over-exerted myself on Worzel Gummidge, my next job was even more strenuous – a three-month UK tour of the musical *Calamity Jane*. Producer Duncan Weldon originally wanted me to do *Annie Get Your Gun*, but Emile Littler, who owned the rights, refused permission for us to do it.

Calamity Jane was more physical than anything I'd ever done. I had to learn how to use a whip, how to twirl guns round my fingers, and jump onto a real stagecoach.

Mummy came to see the show at Brighton. Afterwards she came backstage to my dressing room, with tears in her eyes: 'Oh Babs, I wish I'd never taken you away from the convent!' It was a familiar refrain.

Towards the end of the tour, while we were in Nottingham, Ronnie phoned early one morning, which was a rare enough occurrence, so I sensed there was something wrong.

'What is it? What's wrong?'

'It's yer mother. She's been acting a bit strange, not her usual self,' he said. 'But don't say anything to her.'

When I arrived home late on the Saturday, Ronnie kissed me hello and started fussing round me, which immediately aroused my suspicions. Mummy seemed okay. As it was late, I decided to say nothing.

'What's all this about, Ronnie?' I asked him next morning, 'What's been going on?'

'I think your mother's on some silly pills. She keeps on imagining things.'

'Like what?' I was beginning to smell a rat.

'Well, she reckons she saw me in our bed with this girl.'

'What girl? Are you telling me she saw you in bed with a girl?'

'I told you, take no notice, she's . . .'

I didn't stay to hear the rest. I told my mother what Ronnie had said. She looked embarrassed but said nothing.

'Come on, Mummy. I've got to know what's going on in my own house.'

'I can't tell, Babs. He said he'd chuck me out if I did.'

'But he's already told me about you seeing a girl, so you might as well tell me everything.'

Reluctantly she began:

'I heard these noises coming from upstairs at about three o'clock in the morning. So I went up to see what was happening and that's when I saw them in bed. I was horrified and asked Ronnie what he was about. He certainly didn't expect to see me. He said, "Oh, blimey, we've been found out." Then this blonde got out of bed, grabbed whatever she could, and, laughing like a drain, rushed past me and made for the front door. I followed her downstairs and saw her run up the road, get into a car and drive off. I hardly recognized Ronnie, he was so drunk. He kept saying, "Don't tell Barbara or you'll never live here again." Next morning he was crying, "Rosie, Rosie I'm sorry, I only love Barbara. I was drunk. I didn't know what I was doing."'

Mummy then told him to forget about it. That would have been an end to the story if Ronnie hadn't phoned me.

I mulled the whole thing over during the next few days. I couldn't believe Ronnie would be stupid enough to take a girl to our home, sleep with her in our bed, with his mother-in-law in the house. Yet why would she make up a story like that? There had been many times when I'd answered the phone and the caller had hung up on hearing my voice. And, why did Ronnie seem so amenable to my being on tour this time? What really convinced me Ronnie was being unfaithful was what the little girl who walked my dog said to me:

'Oh, I met your sister.'

'My sister?'

'Yes, I came to take Blue out for a walk and your husband answered the door, and there was a woman sitting inside. I could see through the glass windows. She had on a skirt split right up the side. I just thought it was your sister because of the blonde hair.'

'That's probably my Ronnie's sister,' I told her.

But Ronnie's sister had dark hair, and would never have been dressed that way.

Calamity Jane was in its early stages then, and I was too preoccupied to dwell on this incident. Ronnie and I were doing little more than co-habiting now, and we certainly no longer trusted each other. While I was doing the *Worzel Gummidge* episode I'd met Jon Pertwee's manager, Robert Dunn, who had come to see me several times during the *Calamity Jane* tour. He owned a restaurant in Southampton and he soon made it plain that he wanted to manage me. I was very attracted to him – we soon became lovers – but I wasn't sure I needed a manager. I'd survived all my professional life without one.

Towards the end of the tour, I began feeling sick. I put it down to the long, exhausting run, but Eric Flynn, my leading man, diagnosed something completely different: 'You seem to live on ice cream and Coca-Cola. Are you sure you're not pregnant?' I made a joke of it, but after a week I was no better, so Eric recommended a theatrical doctor he knew well.

'I think I might be pregnant,' I blurted out.

'It's highly unlikely,' he said. 'How old are you?'

'Forty-two.'

He did a test and it proved positive. I was going to have a baby.

The doctor referred me to a psychiatrist, who inquired about the state of my marriage. His advice was that it would be unwise to go ahead, especially in view of my age. Before I knew it, arrangements had been made for me to have an abortion.

I did my two shows the day of my consultation, then travelled home to Ronnie. By that time Ronnie and I had no sex life to speak of – there'd been just this one occasion on a Sunday morning. And now I was pregnant! So I thought: Ronnie and I are meant to be together. I had a feeling the pregnancy was an omen. But this time there was no fuss, no welcome kiss. Instead he was cold, distant and indifferent.

'What are you doing here?' was all he said.

'I wanted to talk to you.'

He just shrugged his shoulders.

'I want to talk about us.'

But he didn't want to know. A baby would obviously make no difference to our marriage. Next morning I returned to Nottingham. I had my abortion and I never even told him.

During the final week of the tour I developed pneumonia. I felt sure it was a result of the abortion. It left me only a few days to recover before rehearsals started at Richmond for *Dick Whittington*. My first break was Christmas Day and I assumed I'd spend New Year's Eve with Ronnie. But when I called him, it was obvious he didn't want me there. So I had a few drinks after the pantomime and stopped off at a pub on the way home to call Ronnie and wish him a Happy New Year. We were within a few miles of each other and I thought of all the other New Year's Eves we'd spent together at the club. I was miserable.

That night I made up my mind to leave him for the second time. Over the years I'd stayed with Ronnie partly because I thought he needed me, that he couldn't cope without me. Now I felt he didn't need me any more. I'd never been allowed to pursue my own relationships because it didn't suit him. Now it did suit him. So he'd obviously found someone. If that's what he wanted, so be it.

Next day I went on my own to look for somewhere to live. I found a place in Knightsbridge, a small basement studio flat near where John Reid was living in Montpellier Square in palatial splendour.

I got the go-ahead to move into the flat on 16 January. I put our house on the market. All I needed to do now was tell Ronnie. I decided to do this on the day of my departure.

7

It was 16 January 1980, the day I'd intended telling Ronnie I was leaving him for good. Over the years the police had arrived at wherever we were living at least once a year. But this time it was obviously much more serious. In a few brief moments my home had been ripped apart and my life shattered. I knew Ronnie was no angel but what could he possibly have done to deserve this invasion of armed policemen with tracker dogs at five o'clock in the morning?

I was left shocked and shaking, but I was sure of one thing: I had to forget my grievances and concentrate all my efforts on helping Ronnie. Whatever heartache we'd caused each other, I remembered I'd made a vow to stand by him for better or worse when we married, and that's what I intended to do. I needed to speak to someone who dealt with criminal cases, so I called Anthony Blok, a solicitor we'd once used when Ronnie got nicked for drunken driving. He agreed to take it on.

Blok managed to track Ronnie down to West Central

police station, Savile Row. The police would not say why they were holding him. I thought of the dust the police had scraped from the bottom of our wardrobe and placed in an envelope. Could it have been some form of drug? There was a drug rehabilitation centre above Ronnie's club. Perhaps someone had off-loaded drugs in the club?

I was desperate for some moral support and it lifted my spirits to see Robert Dunn backstage at Richmond Theatre that night. I was due to call Blok at 11 pm after the curtain had come down on *Dick Whittington* to learn the precise nature of the charges. I remember hearing him say 'murder and arson', but not a lot else – because I passed out.

Thank God for Robert! I hadn't eaten for two days. My brain seemed to have ceased functioning normally. I couldn't go home and face my mother, so Robert booked me into a hotel. I knew I had to pull myself together. In my present state I was as much use to Ronnie as a pork chop at a Jewish wedding. That morning I was due to appear again on Pete Murray's *Open House* radio programme. I called my co-star in the pantomime, Dickie Henderson, hoping he might take my place. He felt I should face the public as soon as possible: 'Go out there, hold your head up high, that's what our business is all about!' I could take that from Dickie because I knew what he'd been through with his wife's suicide.

When I arrived for the broadcast I put on outsize glasses because my eyes were red and swollen from crying, and then brazened it out with the Press, who were circling round me like vultures as I entered the building. The next day there was a horrific picture of me on the front page beside one of Ronnie handcuffed to a policeman. From the Press reports I learnt that Ronnie and his brother, Johnny, were two of nine men arrested in a series of dawn raids, on information supplied by a supergrass.

Later Blok told me that Johnny had been released from police custody and someone called Nicholas Gerard, unknown to me, was being charged with Ronnie for the murder of Alfredo Zomparelli. Gerard was already in prison for armed robbery at the time.

Ronnie had been right all along about Johnny and himself being prime suspects for the Italian's murder. I became more resolved than ever to help prove Ronnie's innocence. The arson was at the Director's Club in Drummond Street, Euston, in 1976, some two years after Zomparelli's murder. For this Ronnie was also charged, together with his business partner, Micky Regan. The Press descended on me again at Richmond Theatre. I told them how sure I was of his innocence and that I believed in 'my old man'.

My biggest worry was not the Press so much as the audience: how would they react to the news that the star of the show was married to a man being charged with murder? I was trembling with fright as I waited to make my big entrance. I needn't have worried. They stood up, cheered and called out my name. I was almost washed away on a wave of goodwill. When it died down I said, 'I'm Dick Whittington now, okay, so let's get on with it!' I continued to get standing ovations at every performance. Little did the punters realize how much it meant to me and how it gave me strength to fight for Ronnie's release.

My solicitor warned me that Ronnie would be remanded in custody with little or no chance of bail. Even so, he advised me to make a list of people who might stand bail just in case the opportunity arose. In the event, Ronnie was sent to Brixton prison on £250,000 bail.

I was allowed to visit him on his birthday, 20 January, taking with me a huge birthday card and a single red rose. I used all my acting skills to confront the Press outside the prison gates, and again inside, for Ronnie's benefit. He was totally dependent on me for moral support and I was touched by the tender letters he wrote from Brixton. I forgot all the bad times because I knew I had to be strong and supportive for both of us.

Meanwhile, wanting to keep it in the family as much as possible, I worked on the list of people who'd stand for bail, with Ronnie's wealthy brother-in-law, Tony Chatwell, at the top of the list – his brothers Johnny and Jimmy were not allowed. For the rest, I reckoned I could raise five to ten grand from my friends in the business. I gave the list to Anthony Blok.

I was living on my nerves. It was like a raging toothache throughout my entire body. Blok insisted I called him at particular times during the day. There were no phonecards then, so I carried vast amounts of loose change wherever I went. Nine times out of ten, the nearest call box would be out of order or occupied.

Johnny drove me to Blok's office and we looked at the names of those willing to stand bail. There was one name conspicuous by its absence.

'Where's Tony Chatwell, my brother-in-law?' demanded Johnny.

'I'm sorry, he won't stand bail,' replied Blok.

Johnny and I were mortified. Ronnie had always been close to his sister, Patsy, Tony Chatwell's wife. We'd been on holiday with her and Tony in Spain, and when they'd had a bit of trouble with their marriage, their kids came to stay with us. Frantic now to make up the difference, I called up a lot of people close to me. But they all found some excuse.

Johnny drove me back to Richmond Theatre for the evening show. The traffic was nose-to-tail, the skies were dark, and it was raining. But nothing was gloomier or more congested than my head on that Black Monday. The stage doorman gave me his usual cheery greeting, but I charged straight past him without saying a word. Usually it was ''Allo Joe, how's it going?' My black mood obviously didn't go unnoticed because a few minutes later, Dickie Henderson came along to my dressing room. 'Not feeling too good tonight, honey?' I put my arms around him and sighed, 'Oh Dickie . . .' Then I blurted out the day's events. 'Now I've got to go out there and be Barbara Windsor! It's the last thing I feel like!' Dickie talked to me like a kindly uncle. 'You've got some bad troubles now,' he said, 'I know what it's like, I've been there myself. But if you just get out there, it'll be okay.'

After the show, Dickie put his head round the door. I said, 'You're right, darling, it did help me to forget . . . but it's coming back to your dressing room after!'

Over the next week I tried to get to Tony Chatwell, to find out why he'd let us down. The au pair answered the phone every time, and neither he nor Ronnie's sister ever bothered to call me back. In exasperation I said to the au pair, 'Can you give him this message: if he doesn't call me tomorrow, I shall be outside Mr Chatwell's factory with a banner telling the whole world he won't stand bail for his own brother-in-law. Tell him he is Ronnie Knight's brother-in-law!' He came round next morning at nine o'clock. I didn't even offer him a glass of water. He was sweating like a pig. He said it would be bad for business for him to be associated with Ronnie, but that he'd try to find someone else to stand bail. I never spoke to him or Patsy again.

Back to square one. I knew I could ask John Reid and his client Elton John, both wealthy men, but I didn't want to abuse our friendship. The next day Peter Charlesworth, my former agent, contacted me and offered to help, restoring my faith in human nature. Anna Karen ain't got nothing. All she's got is her house. She offered me that. Then right out of the blue, Harry and Phyllis Hewson, good friends of mine from Birmingham, phoned. Harry was in business and I had opened some shops for him. I always stayed with his family when I was in Birmingham. I didn't really want to discuss my problems, but Harry insisted. When I told him of the difficulties in raising bail, Harry said I could count him in to the tune of £100,000. His wife, Phyllis, and her son-in-law David offered a further sum to the same value. No words could express my gratitude to these wonderful people.

I was wondering where to turn for the remaining £50,000 when Robert Dunn, offered me the lease of his cottage. I was overwhelmed.

At last we were able to apply for bail. Twice it was turned down at Bow Street magistrates court, thanks to police opposition. The next remand hearing would be at Lambeth court. This time luck was on our side. Firstly, the police failed to arrive on time, having got stuck in a traffic jam, and secondly, the magistrate, Ralph Lownie, I knew from Anthony Blok, was more likely to give us a fair hearing. The entire case against Ronnie had been built up on the evidence of the supergrass Bradshaw and this particular magistrate had a great distrust of informers. He asked to see the people willing to put up £250,000. Only two were present, but Mr Lownie said bail would be granted if the others came to court the following day. I couldn't believe my ears. You should have seen the looks the police gave us!

The next day, 1 February 1980, bail was agreed on condition that Ronnie handed in his passport. Micky Regan, who was only on an arson charge, was allowed out on £20,000 bail.

I went up to Brixton next morning. We were besieged by what seemed like the entire media world as Ronnie emerged from the gates, looking thin but otherwise well. He told the Press he'd taken up smoking inside because of the pressure. When they asked him what he was going to do, with a typical Ronnie remark he just said, 'Go home and have a bath.'

I'd made arrangements for us all to have a drink at the Savoy, so he could have a bit of high life after being locked up in a poky prison cell. We were joined by all the people who had stood bail.

It was the last night of *Dick Whittington* at Richmond, and I persuaded Ronnie to bring my mother along afterwards for a celebration. You can imagine how relieved I felt after all the traumas, and how grateful I was to Dickie Henderson and the others for helping me through it. It was some party!

After Ronnie's release I took our house off the market. Stanmore was familiar ground to Ronnie and he needed a port in a storm. He also needed me more than ever before. Adversity had thrown us back into each other's arms, and I felt closer to him than I had done for years.

He had to appear in court every month for a review of his bail. At the June hearing we heard he would be committed for trial on 14 July. I turned down a lot of work that summer because I didn't feel I could give it my full attention. But I took on Robert Dunn as my manager and he talked me into doing another week's filming on *Worzel Gummidge*. As I say, I didn't really feel I needed a manager but Robert was so kind to me, driving me around and giving me much-needed moral support.

After the filming on *Worzel Gummidge*, there was a party in Hampshire where I met up with Robert. I was anxious to get home to Ronnie, but Robert insisted on staying till the end. On the way back Robert's car landed in a ditch. I was badly shaken but we struggled home somehow and I got in about two in the morning, covered with blood. When I tried to explain the accident to Ronnie he wouldn't listen. He was furious with me for being so late.

Next morning, hardly able to move, I was rushed off to hospital where it was discovered that I had sustained serious internal injuries. After a week in hospital I had a relapse and required emergency surgery. It was touch and go whether I would come out of the operating theatre alive.

Ronnie came to see me every day in hospital. Always looking so glamorous, he became the ward's pin-up boy. The doctors were not at all pleased when I discharged myself, and they told me to take it easy, but how could I? I put our house on the market again because I was now convinced it was the cause of all this never-ending bad fortune.

All my thoughts were now focussed on Ronnie's trial. Whatever my state of health, I was determined to be there on 14 July. Every night I prayed the case against him would be dropped so that this cloud hanging over our lives would be lifted once and for all. Knowing and loving Ronnie like I did, I was sure he had nothing to do with Zomparelli's murder. How could I be living with a man capable of murder? It wasn't possible. The trial was at Lambeth magistrates' court. We had lunch at a nearby pub beforehand and when it was time to go, Ronnie put some money on the table and said, 'That's for the lunch. You stay here. I'll see you when I come out of court.' He told me later he wanted to remember me having a nice time, because he knew that his bail would be withdrawn if the case was sent for trial at a higher court.

The hearing lasted three days. Bradshaw claimed Ronnie set up the murder of Zomparelli, paying him and Nicholas Gerard to carry it out. My hopes that the case would be dismissed were soon dashed. Both he and Gerard were committed to trial by jury at the Old Bailey. Bail was withdrawn, as the police feared Ronnie would interfere with witnesses or abscond.

The full horror of it all struck home that evening when I went to see Ronnie. For the first time in my life I saw my husband behind bars, in a small, dingy prison cell. A small window high on the wall, heavily barred, let in the light of day, but only just. I'd always thought British justice believed every man innocent until he is proven guilty. It looked to me as if this man were already convicted. I felt like baking him a cake with a file in it!

I was surprised to find Ronnie quite relaxed. 'We must do everything we can to get my bail back,' he said, and I assured him he could count on me to do everything in my power.

To help me relax and recover fully from the car

accident, Johnny and his wife, Diane, invited me to go with them to Spain and the villa we shared in Benal Madena. Though they were kindness itself, I couldn't relax knowing there was still so much to be done for Ronnie. I returned home to try to obtain bail for Ronnie through the Court of Appeal. But it was not to be.

Ronnie's trial was eventually fixed for 10 November 1980. I visited him every day and took his favourite food in with me. He used to take extra potatoes and Yorkshire puddings when I did roast beef so he could share them out among his inmates. I was allowed to take him a quarter bottle of red wine. Even though we saw each other frequently, he wrote me loving letters full of endearments and optimism. I kept every one of them. He also made me a parchment scroll.

'Even though we live far from each other, Barbra, I always talk to you in my thoughts and see you in my dreams. It doesn't matter that we are not together because our love is such a strong part of my life. As long as I know you are happy where you are, I too am happy. I am your husband and my love for you goes deep, Barbra. There is nothing I can give you which you have not got, but there is much, while I cannot give it, you can take. You know that nothing can ever change what we have always been, and always will be to each other, Barbra.'

Ronnie had spelled my name wrong!

He felt optimistic about the outcome of the trial, because he knew jurors do not like to base their verdict on the evidence of one witness. As long as the prosecution had no corroborating witness, Ronnie reckoned he was okay. There was no shortage of friends and family visiting him, but he always said the same thing to me: 'I like you coming best, Bar.'

I could never decide what to wear when I visited Ronnie. I didn't want to overdress in case they thought I was pulling the big star act, but obviously I wanted to look nice for him. I think Ronnie felt proud of me, because the prison officers would say things to him like, 'No airs and graces, your missus, she talks to everyone.'

Being a familiar face in a place like that always causes a bit of a stir. People would come over and ask for my autograph or confide their ambitions of going on the stage. One Irish girl did an impromptu audition for me – her rendition of *Molly Malone*. At times the whole thing was like a black comedy by Joe Orton!

With all the publicity Ronnie's case received I wasn't spared the attention of cranks. When you are a public person they know how to find you, so I got all these bogus phone calls from men saying they had information that would help my husband. They obviously got a kick out of putting me in a compromising position. One guy gave me an address in Camden Town and told me to meet him there at one o'clock in the morning. As he swore he had information that could help Ronnie, I decided to risk it. I know, you're thinking I was barmy, and there are no prizes for guessing that he didn't turn up. No doubt the perverted bugger was lurking in a shop window somewhere nearby, taking his pleasure out of making somebody famous look a complete prat. But I never knew when it might be for real.

It wasn't the only time I went on a wild goose chase in the hope of turning up some concrete evidence, but none of them yielded anything worth hearing. I had to face up to the fact that Ronnie could be sentenced to 20 years which might be reduced to ten or even eight years if he behaved himself. I'd already decided what to do if the worst came to the worst. I would sell the house, buy a smaller one and invest the difference in a business for Ronnie when he came out. Thinking along these lines sent shivers down my spine, but it did help me to develop a more positive approach to the trial.

As November approached he became low. Having been locked up for three months, he felt no different to the other prisoners. His self-confidence had flown out of the window and his nerves were shot to pieces.

'Isn't it amazing,' he said to me on one visit, 'in a few days' time I could be serving 20 years?'

'You must think positive,' I told him, 'You'll be back home with me, and that's an end to it!'

The lack of a corroborating witness was the one thing we could count on. Bradshaw was a self-confessed criminal. Anything he said in court would be open to dispute and contradiction.

On the Friday before the trial began I was summoned to my solicitor's office. The police had handed over the documents and files that made up their case. Anthony Blok turned to me with a long face: 'Barbara, we're in deep trouble. The police have managed to find a corroborating witness.'

He was called Gerald Knight and his name had been withheld until the last possible moment to prevent us from checking him out. He was no relation to Ronnie. I had met him when Ronnie and I lived in Hendon. Gerry, as I knew him, used to bring us new-laid eggs and, at one time, he and Ronnie were considering buying a joint property in Hertfordshire. During negotiations he gave me a £5,000 cheque to cash and it bounced. We never saw him again after that.

Blok leafed through some papers and said, 'Just as I thought! It says here that Gerald Knight insists he never met Ronnie. Now if we can prove that he did by producing the cheque that bounced, we could discredit him as a witness.'

I couldn't wait to get home and find the cheque. Being a meticulous sort of person I knew exactly where to lay my hands on it. Before I left, Blok suggested we hire a private detective to dig something up on Gerry Knight. All we knew about him was that, like Bradshaw, he too was serving a prison sentence and probably willing to tell any old story in order to get remission.

Back at the house in Stanmore I began my frantic search for the cheque. One thing bothered me. In the move from Hendon to Stanmore I had disposed of a great deal of paperwork. I remembered placing the cheque in a large envelope where I put all Ronnie's IOU's and any cheques that bounced from his club. I went directly to the drawer containing everything connected with the business and found the envelope. To my horror, all the cheques were there except Gerry Knight's. I kept telling myself it must be there. I wouldn't have singled out one item to throw away. Beside myself with panic, I emptied everything on the floor. Then I went up to the loft and did the same. My mother thought I'd gone raving mad. I never swore at my mother but now I screamed at her to piss off. I felt like a time-bomb about to go off.

In the midst of this misery Ronnie's brother Jimmy phoned to ask me about Gerry Knight. As we were saying goodbye, he said, 'You must prepare yourself, Bar. Ron could get at least 25 years.' That finished me off. I raced around the house like a caged animal looking in all the rooms, examining every item of clothing, every pocket, even things I'd worn the day before! In the end I flopped on the floor, totally exhausted. Only Mummy's cajoling got me into bed. 'With a clear head, you'll know where to look in the morning,' she said, calmly.

I started from scratch in the morning. Returning to my desk I yanked the drawer right out in frustration. Stuck at the back was a small manilla envelope containing Gerry Knight's cheque. Mummy came running when she heard my screams of delight. It was our trump card and Blok swore me to secrecy. I couldn't even tell Ronnie because there were no Sunday visits.

The trial opened on Monday, 10 November 1980 in No. 1 Court of the Old Bailey, the scene of so many celebrated criminal proceedings. It seemed unreal that my husband, my Ronnie, was fighting for his freedom in this place where so many evil criminals had been tried. Being a witness against Gerry Knight meant I must stay away from the court until it was time for me to give evidence. Blok asked me to do a disappearing act. He could not risk the prosecution or the police rumbling what we had up our sleeves.

This caused a dilemma. It was common knowledge that I never missed a day in court when Ronnie was remanded in custody. The Press would soon smell a rat if I wasn't around. We needed a legitimate excuse for my absence. God was in his heaven that day because, when I got home, there was a message to say I was needed for an extra couple of days filming on *Worzel Gummidge*. So there was Windsor, charging around on runners for two days before giving the performance of her life at the Old Bailey!

On the first day of the case I attended Hattie Jacques's memorial service at St Paul's, Covent Garden, and I was still dressed in black when I visited Ronnie in his cell at the Old Bailey. Naturally enough, he found it hard to concentrate on anything other than the case.

'I've been to Hattie's funeral,' I told him.

'Really? How was she?'

'Dead,' I replied.

I was due to give evidence. As I was waiting to go into court, the private detective we'd hired to check out Gerry Knight gave me some useful advice: 'For what it's worth, don't volunteer any information. Just answer "yes" or "no".'

I felt as nervous as a kitten. You'd think after all my years in showbusiness, it would have been a piece of cake. But this was different. This time I was putting myself on show and I'd have nobody writing my dialogue.

Just as I was called a man tapped me on the shoulder and said: 'Do you know your husband's got another woman?'

I tried to make light of it: 'Of course I know . . . he's got at least half a dozen!'

It should have fazed me, but all it did was to strengthen my resolve to do all I could to help Ronnie. Everything else seemed unimportant.

Next thing I knew I was standing in the witness box. In front of me was an array of clerks, officials and barristers in their wigs and gowns. Our barrister, Ivor Richards, gave me a friendly nod. The judge looked at me blankly. I suppose he'd never seen a *Carry On*! The jurors were close to the witness box and I noticed that two of the 12 were women. I smiled nervously at Ronnie in the dock and he gave me a look that said, 'I'm depending on you, Babs.' There was a buzz in the public gallery, which contained many of our friends. I had this lovely feeling that they were on our side, like the audience at the Richmond panto.

Our barrister referred to me as Mrs Knight. The prosecuting counsel called me Miss Windsor. I was about to correct him when I remembered the private detective's words about keeping quiet. The judge intervened. 'Well, which is she? What are you going to call her? Miss Windsor or Mrs Knight?' He sounded grumpy and impatient. This time I did speak up: 'Sir, I'd like to be called Mrs Knight. I am Mrs Knight!' I knew I'd said the right thing, but I was soon knocked off my perch by the prosecution, asking if I was aware that armed robbers used Ronnie's A & R club. They were referring to Nicky Gerard.

'My husband never told me so,' I replied. 'All sorts of people use it. It's not confined to any particular kind of person.'

Then they brought in Gerry Knight. He claimed he had heard Ronnie talk about a death contract on Zomparelli. Ronnie wanted Zomparelli buried, he said, and would supply Nicky Gerard with the gun to kill him.

During cross-examination our counsel asked Knight if he had ever met the defendant. He said he hadn't. He also denied having had any transactions with Ronnie. Mr Richards asked Knight what he would say if his cheque for £5,000 made out to Ronald Knight could be produced. Then the cheque was held up for everyone to see – and

Gerry Knight's credibility fell to pieces. We'd clobbered the corroborating witness!

To Ronnie each day's hearing resembled a boxing match. Round one to us, round two to them, and so on. That day's was a real knockout.

The following day, having finished giving my evidence, I sat at the back of the court with Robert Dunn, my manager. When I went to see Ronnie later, he said: 'I didn't see you in court today . . . where were you?' I told him I was sitting at the back. 'That's no good. You must sit in the public gallery where I can see you.' So, the next day, I stood in the pouring rain with a lot of strangers and struggled up the long flight of stone steps to the public gallery in order to keep him happy. I'd never really had time to get over my accident, so it began to take its toll after a few days. I was so relieved when a friend offered to stand in the queue for me, ensuring me a good place in the front row of the gallery in full view of Ronnie and the jury.

When I first saw Nicky Gerard, I couldn't believe how young he was, at least 20 years younger than Ronnie. I couldn't believe Ronnie would go around with someone that young. It was only a little thing, but it made me believe in Ronnie's innocence more strongly.

The bills for the case were enormous, and Ronnie was receiving very little legal aid. So, against our better judgement, we signed a contract for an exclusive with the *Sunday Mirror*. They booked me into the Hilton for the duration of the trial, and Robert drove me to the Old Bailey every day, which ensured I was always on time.

For the next ten days I sat in the gallery from ten o'clock in the morning till four in the afternoon, with a break for lunch. To get a good view of the proceedings I had to lean forward on my hard wooden bench. Ronnie is a quiet man by nature and there were no heated outbursts, but I could always detect signs of hope, relief or sometimes elation when things were going well, anguish and dejection when the prosecution gained the upper hand. He'd never been much of a communicator, but we developed an odd sort of telepathy during the trial.

On the day the prosecution summed up the case against him, I saw Ronnie's face twisted with utter despair. Some horrific things were said about him and Gerard; it all sounded so real and persuasive. Even the judge's interventions seemed to add weight to the prosecution case.

Blok advised me to tell Ronnie that that was as bad as it would get. From then on, things would start to look more hopeful.

Ronnie was in a black mood that evening: 'That's it, that's the end. They're going to find me guilty! I'd rather top meself.'

No amount of reassurance from me seemed to make any difference. If anything it made things worse. 'You'll have to divorce me, Bar. Go out there and start a new life. Forget all about me . . .'

I grabbed hold of him. 'Pull yourself together! They've heard all the bad things! Our barrister has the last word, that's what the jury will hear before they retire.'

I felt near to collapse when I got to the court with the *Sunday Mirror* reporter Gill Preece on the day of the verdict. Inside they told me to sit in the courtroom itself. Only Robert Dunn was allowed to sit with me. Whatever the verdict, they wanted me to make a quick exit to a small room outside. Mr Richards summed up for the defence in the morning. When the court reconvened after lunch, the jury had already reached their verdict. I've never been so frightened in my life. I couldn't stop shaking. I felt as if I were on trial myself.

I suppose the judge spoke, then the foreman of the jury . . . but I heard nothing. After a while I was aware of a hubbub and Robert had his arm round my shoulder. The next thing I knew, it was all over; Robert and I were in a tiny little room like a cupboard adjoining the court. Once it sunk in that both Ronnie and Nicky Gerard had been cleared of the murder charge, the flood-gates opened. I couldn't stop crying.

When I went to the cells beneath the courtroom to fetch Ronnie I found him in tears, too. We just clung to each other! It was the happiest day of my life. The terrible cloud that had been hanging over us all these months was finally blown away. I felt light-headed with relief, but we were both too drained to celebrate.

The next day we heard that Ronnie and Micky Regan had also been cleared of the arson charge.

Nicky Gerard returned to prison, where he was serving out the rest of his time. He wrote to us saying he hadn't stopped smiling since the acquittal. 'When I got back to Wormwood Scrubs everyone was cheering and slapping me on the back . . . I must be the happy-go-luckiest prisoner in England.'

Gerard also said that Bradshaw, the supergrass, had been publicly discredited by the Director of Public Prosecutions, who vowed never to rely on his evidence again.

It was time to begin a new chapter.

8

The minute Ronnie was released, the Press began camping outside our house in Stanmore. The *Sunday Mirror* was anxious that we keep everyone else at bay until their 'exclusive' had appeared on the Sunday.

We drove out to the country with Robert Dunn and his girlfriend, Lynn. After the deprivations of recent months, Ronnie was ready to let his hair down, ordering the best wine with our meal. But he was in a strangely black mood. He insisted on driving the car home which, by this time, he was in no state to do. We did all we could to stop him, short of taking the keys away. 'I'm going to drive,' he kept on saying.

The journey back was a nightmare. He drove like a maniac along the narrow country lanes, taking corners too fast, swerving violently, missing oncoming cars by a hair's breadth. I thought he was trying to kill me. God knows how we arrived home in one piece. Without saying a word, Ronnie raced straight upstairs. I couldn't fathom why a man who'd just escaped a 20-year gaol sentence by the skin of his teeth should be in such a vile temper. When I got upstairs I found Ronnie sobbing in the bedroom.

'I'm so fucking unhappy. Our marriage was gone – I nearly lost you. You can make it right, Windsor. You're my whole life.'

'You're home now,' I said. 'We'll wipe out everything that's ever happened. God's given us another chance . . . we're meant to be together.'

Next day I was starting rehearsals for the 1980–81 pantomime season in Newcastle. I'd arranged this way back when he'd first got arrested. Before I left I said, 'Tell you what, why don't we spend Christmas together in Newcastle.'

He said, 'What a good idea!'

I thought I was hearing things. Previous years I always had to rush home to cook the turkey for Christmas Day, then dash back for the show on Boxing Day. Now I was amazed he'd go all the way up North.

We had a smashing time at the Holiday Inn. I was so pickled on Christmas Day that I played the Boxing Day matinée with a colossal hangover. I don't know if it was the notoriety surrounding the case, but we broke all box office records in Newcastle that season.

Ronnie was always very, very prompt. We were due to eat at five o'clock sharp. When he failed to turn up one evening, I called around. He'd been seen at lunchtime but not since. Round about seven o'clock I heard the garage doors open. I ran to see what had happened and found Ronnie still in his car, his head slumped against the window. His whole face was smashed in, his clothing ripped, blood all over the place, and he'd shat in his trousers.

I took his clothes off and chucked them away, then bathed him and put him to bed. He'd been drinking heavily. While I was with him in the bedroom, the phone rang. It was a woman's voice, screaming and crying uncontrollably. I passed the phone to Ronnie. 'No, I'm all right,' he said and put the receiver down.

Was this woman with him when the fight had happened? Was she the cause of it? Who the hell was she? My head was spinning with unanswered questions, but this was no time to start giving him the third degree.

Ronnie and I were due to record a TV programme in the series *Fame* for the BBC, and when John Pitman came to interview us, Ronnie's face was still swollen from the beating he'd taken. I told Pitman he'd walked into a door so we postponed it for a few days to let the swelling go down; in view of the case, I didn't think it would do Ronnie's reputation much good for millions of viewers to see him all beaten up.

I'd never lost touch with Kenny Williams who, since his *Carry On* days, had started directing for the stage. He was a great mate of Joe Orton's up to the time he died so brutally, and Joe had always said to Kenny that he'd love to see me play Kath, the sex-mad landlady, in *Entertaining Mr Sloane*. He said, 'You've got to believe Sloane wants to fuck Kath.' So when Kenny asked me if I'd play Kath at the Lyric Theatre, Hammersmith, I jumped at the chance of working with my old pal. The idea of following in Beryl Reid's footsteps frightened the life out of me, but with lots of help and encouragement from Kenny and another old mate, Dave King, playing my brother, I felt I'd cracked it.

It was during the previews that I returned home one night to find the house had been burgled. There were empty beer cans all around, as if whoever did it had made themselves thoroughly at home. For some reason a knife had been left on top of the piano, and a pair of my knickers on the bed. It was all very strange and disconcerting.

I rushed upstairs to check on the set of drawers where all our money and valuables were kept. One of the drawers had a well-concealed false bottom, but, even so, the money and jewellery had gone from it. All that was left were some worry beads that Robert had brought me back from Greece. Every piece of jewellery had been taken, apart from my wedding ring, which I wore all the time. I'd treasured the diamond ring Sid had given me, a trinket from Danny La Rue, and a bracelet from Frank Sinatra's jeweller in New York. Above all Ronnie had bought me some wonderful stuff over the years. Because of the case the insurance people had refused to insure us. My only consolation was that I had had to sell a number of pieces to help cover costs. Even so I estimated the loss at around £60,000.

Ronnie was furious that I informed the police before I called him. He raced home before they arrived and refused to let the CID into the house. He kept saying, 'They're only possessions, we'll get them back.' He even refused to let the police take fingerprints. His behaviour was inexplicable. All he said was 'What's gone is gone,' as if that was any consolation.

Not long after the burglary I collapsed during a performance of *Entertaining Mr Sloane*. I woke up in an oxygen tent. I thought my collapse had just been an aberration of some sort, but when the play ended, I took a short break in Spain. It was then I learnt that it was a symptom of a much deeper malaise.

As I stepped from the plane at Malaga airport, I just froze on the spot. I couldn't move a limb. Eventually with Ronnie's help I shuffled into the arrival lounge. Once we got to the villa, the opposite happened. I couldn't sit still. If I stood up, I wanted to sit down. I felt sick but wasn't. My body and brain were in turmoil. During one bad attack of nausea, I went to see a doctor. He said I was seriously run down and needed some vitamin pills. I felt like an amputee being offered a walking stick. My condition worsened that night.

I was getting ready to go to bed when everything disintegrated. It was as if my body was completely giving up. As I stood up everything streamed out of my nose, bowels and bladder. I saw the look of horror on Ronnie's face.

'Bar, what's happening to you?' he said.

There was no question of flying home to England and, although we'd always agreed Spanish hospitals were best avoided, that's where we finished up. I was lying there not speaking a word of Spanish, trying to explain my life story, to make them understand why things had gone wrong. Eventually I managed to talk to a German doctor who spoke English. He diagnosed a nervous breakdown. It was clear to me then that it was a delayed reaction to the trauma of the trial five months previously.

I'd spent two days in hospital when I became agitated and asked Ronnie to take me back to England. Once he had escorted me back, he returned to Spain, saying he had business to attend to.

I knew I had to pull myself together. I was

contracted to do a summer season of *The Mating Game* in Blackpool, with Trevor Bannister and Jack Smethurst.

During rehearsals we did a Press call to promote the show. I agreed to this on condition that I wasn't quizzed about Ronnie. They stuck to their promise, all except one reporter who stayed behind after the others had gone.

'Do you know your husband is having an affair with a barmaid called Susan Haylock?' she said. 'They're in Spain together now.'

I tried to laugh it off with some throwaway quip, but it had been like sticking a knife into my stomach and twisting the blade. I did my best to convince myself that the rotten cow had said it out of spite, or simply to satisfy some ravenous news editor, but really I felt like running away somewhere and bursting into tears. I told Trevor Bannister who tried to reassure me it was just the Press up to their old tricks again.

I felt better until the paper was delivered the next morning. On the front page was a big picture of my Ronnie saying, 'Yes I do employ a girl called Susan Haylock – but Barbara is the only one in my life. I love her.'

Before *The Mating Game* opened, I did a charity show in Blackpool where I'd been evacuated as a child; now my name was up in lights. In the presence of Prince Charles I sang a medley of Marie Lloyd numbers from *Sing a Rude Song*. Afterwards they came backstage to meet the cast. When my turn came to be introduced, the Prince looked at me and said: 'Is everything all right now?' He was obviously referring to Ronnie's case, and I was really chuffed that he should take the trouble to ask.

I continued to feel unwell thoughout the Blackpool season, and the press wouldn't leave me alone. They

*Carry On
Again . . .*

Above: *Sid James, Joan Sims, Peter Rogers, Gerald Thomas, Charles Hawtrey, Kenneth Williams, Hattie Jacques, Jim Dale*

Opposite above: *Chrissie and Mickey Regan, me and Ronnie and Maureen and Freddie Foreman*

Opposite below: *In my dressing-room during the run of 'Come Spy with Me' with Noel Coward, Danny La Rue and Rudolph Nureyev*

On the set of 'The Boyfriend'
with Ronnie

In 'The Threepenny Opera'
with Vanessa Redgrave

In 'Dick Whittington'

Above: *With Maurice Gibb during the run of 'Marie Lloyd'*

With John Reid

The Merry Wives of Windsor

On my way into Leman Street Police Station to be questioned about Ronnie

*It might sound daft but
when you're deeply in love
and happy with someone
age doesn't come into it*

Above: *Outside The Ploug
Inn*

Left: *On honeymoon in
Jamaica*

were far more interested in my relationship with Ronnie than *The Mating Game*. On top of that I had John Pitman's television crew following me around. They even filmed Robert Dunn attempting to deal with the Press at the stage door.

Ronnie was late back from Spain. He called me on my birthday to wish me many happy returns.

'What's so fucking happy about it?' I said.

'What's the matter?'

'You should be here with me, convincing me it isn't true. I would've done that for you.'

A couple of days later he joined me in Blackpool, looking relaxed and suntanned. In stark contrast I'd lost a lot of weight and those famous Windsor boobs had shrunk beyond recognition. My face was hardly any better. Ronnie was visibly shaken.

'My God,' he said when he saw me, 'What's wrong with you?'

All the symptoms of a nervous breakdown were back. I was getting panic attacks on stage. I was terrified to go out there. The day before Ronnie's arrival I'd felt so bad I didn't go on. I was told by the doctor that I must take exercise, but I couldn't. When Ronnie arrived he had to help me get around and cook meals for me. My understudy was taken ill. It looked as if the show would have to come off. To placate the producer, I went back on stage, only to have another relapse. I felt desperate. Then Ronnie left again for Spain.

'What can I do?' I asked my doctor. 'I simply cannot face the stage again tonight.'

He said there were two options. Either he could give me something to get me through the show or he could put me on a train home. 'Only you can say how important it is to do the show.'

I hate to let people down. I'm a trooper at heart. I asked him to give me something to take. I did the show, and the rest of the three weeks that were left. But the thought that lodged in my mind was that it was the first time my private life had taken over my work.

That autumn I decided to accept an offer on the Stanmore house – the robbery had somehow tainted the place for me. We were given a moving date in October. I just had time to go to Spain to visit Ronnie before leaving for Australia to do a talk show. I was missing Ronnie and I wanted him to sort it all out.

At the airport I bought some extra holiday insurance to safeguard myself against further illness. The lady on the counter recognized me and said: 'Who ever would have thought you'd have trouble in your marriage?' I was about to tell the cheeky cow to mind her own business when she carried on: 'I'll never forget that night in the club at Ruislip. These three men went crazy when they saw your husband with some blonde instead of you. They hated seeing him cheating on you after all you did for him, all your loyalty. The drunker they became, the more aggressive they were towards your husband. Finally they laid into him.' She was referring to the night he came home late, all smashed up.

It was amazing. I didn't know this woman from Adam, yet here she was putting the boot into my marriage! Of course it stirred up all my doubts about Ronnie, doubts that burrowed deeper when I arrived in Spain and found a bikini at the villa which didn't belong to me.

In the brief time I was with Ronnie it became clear

that as much as I wanted him to sort it all out, he wanted *me* to sort it all out. Poor Ronnie had nothing now, no club and no money, and he believed that, as always, I would be strong, that I would come and rescue him. He wanted me to be the Barbara of old, but the problem was that after the trauma of the case I didn't have it in me. Above all he wanted our relationship to be like it was years ago, but I was too ill – I'd gone down to six stone – and I was getting older. My relationship with Ronnie was slipping away irrevocably, and the only thing I could cling on to was my career.

I'd been invited to appear on TV in Australia on the prestigious *Mike Walsh Show*. It was an all-expenses paid trip with a stopover in Bali. I couldn't believe it when Ronnie said he wouldn't be coming. Even the prospect of free first-class air travel wasn't enough to tempt him. I was in no fit state to put up a fight. I felt entirely defeated by our marriage and completely alienated from Ronnie. So I went to Australia without him.

The Mike Walsh Show, as I say, is big down under, and guests are given the opportunity to perform if they wish. Mike had asked me to come for the whole week. I talked about the *Carry On*s. Danny La Rue and Wayne King, the pianist, joined me for a couple of Marie Lloyd numbers. It was a wonderful time, but the week was marred for me by thoughts of Ronnie's absence and what he might be getting up to back home. Nor could I get out of my mind what the lady had told me at Heathrow Airport.

Danny suggested I should stop off in Los Angeles on my way home. I was planning to go on to Las Vegas to stay with Liberace, whom I'd met back in London, but when I called Ronnie he told me that Mummy was ill.

Next morning I was on a plane home.

I went straight to the hospital in Canterbury where Mummy was having tests. She was dressed up and looking nice. The ward sister came over and my mother said to her: 'Everything will be all right now. My Babs is home.' That was most unlike Mummy. Normally I couldn't put a foot right.

To add to my worries, our move from Stanmore was imminent and I still hadn't found anywhere to live. So, in between hospital visits, I chased around looking at properties. We wanted an unfurnished place where we could store our things until we knew where to settle for good. A house in Windsor was recommended, which I thought was fabulous. But Ronnie didn't fancy it. 'I'm a north London boy,' was what he said. So we looked at a house in Edgware, which I thought was awful – damp and cold. But Ronnie took a shine to it.

One night while I was still at Stanmore there was a knock on the door. It was my uncle Ronnie and cousin Kenny. Kenny said, 'We've been to see your mother, and we've got some bad news. She doesn't have long to live – three weeks at the most.'

Ronnie happened to ring from a club while they were still there. I told him what they'd said.

'Will you please come home, I need you.'

'No, you'll be alright.'

I put the receiver down. Kenny said, 'Is Ronnie coming home?'

'Oh yeah,' I said.

'Are you sure? We don't want to leave you on your own.'

'I'm fine!'

Ronnie returned at four in the morning.

Then one day on one of my visits, without any preamble, Mummy herself told me she was dying. Apparently a young doctor had picked up her clipboard and said: 'Hmm, this isn't good news for you, is it?' I was furious and made arrangements to remove her straight away. 'Yes, I'd love to,' she said when I asked her if she'd like to stay with us. We got her into the back of the car. Within no time at all she was fast asleep. I looked back. The sun hit her face and she was smiling. She who had been so full of aggravation for most of her life now looked so peaceful.

'I wish she'd go now,' I said to Ronnie.

Never having seen anyone die, I was very frightened. I wasn't sure how I'd cope if anything happened while I was alone. So that evening I asked Ronnie to come home early from a night out with the boys. Even though Mummy was weak, she was full of chat.

We'd fought like cat and mouse all our lives. She'd been domineering, stubborn and just plain nasty at times – perhaps all mother and daughter relationships are like this – but, though she never said it, I think she was proud of me. For better or worse, I was her little Babs.

She squeezed my hand. 'You won't cry, Babs, will you?'

'Cry over you? I should co-co!'

She laughed.

I said, 'I just know what will happen. You'll get better and you'll drive me mental again, just like before!'

Come midnight Ronnie wasn't home. I waited and waited. I was still waiting up at 3 am. I kept going down to the front door and looking out. I couldn't sleep, and was terrified Mummy would slip away while I was out of the room.

Had he had an accident? It was hard to believe Ronnie would willingly stay out late while my mother lay dying. Finally, at 6.30 in the morning, he made an appearance, pissed out of his mind.

'You're a rotten shit!' I spat the words at him. 'Don't you realize Mummy could have died?'

'Well, she didn't, did she?'

The day we were due to move house, Mummy's condition worsened and she had to go back into hospital. I postponed our move to the following day and went with her in the ambulance, while Ronnie followed in the car. She kept asking if he was all right, if he was still behind us.

'He used to be such a good boy,' she said. 'What's happened to him?'

I got this unaccountable urge to defend him. 'Oh Mum! It's six of one and half a dozen of the other. You know what I'm like!'

'No, Babs, I don't think any of this is your doing.'

I spent most of the time at the hospital, despite the move. In the room next to Mummy's was a young guy in a coma who kept screaming out. She said, 'God should take me and let that young man live.'

'Don't be daft,' I told her. 'You'll be out of here soon.'

Because I'm a familiar face there was a constant stream of people asking for autographs and expecting me to be cheerful when, in fact, I was feeling wretched. People don't think of you as Barbara whose mother is dying of cancer. They see the public image and, as we all know, celebrities are public property! I'm told when Eric Morecambe was dying of a heart attack, someone actually came up to ask for his autograph.

I found it very difficult trying to keep myself

together. I stayed by her side after she fell into a coma, because I wanted to be there just in case she came round. But she died without regaining consciousness. There was a huge bunch of roses by her bed, but only one was still alive. I took it from the vase and put it in her hair.

'Cor, doesn't she look beautiful,' Ronnie said when he came to collect me.

My mother had never been an easy person to be with. I only wish I'd once told her I love her – or heard her say she loved me.

After she died I found she'd written me a letter. It began, 'To the most wonderful daughter in the world . . .' A month later I did a TV programme called 'Mothers By Daughters', and talking about this letter made hidden feelings flood to the surface. I realized that, even if she'd never actually said it, she'd always loved me, and, even though it often seemed she wanted to keep me down, she'd always had my best interests at heart.

I plunged into work. Even though my heart was broken, I didn't have time to grieve. I had to go to Nottingham to start rehearsals for Aladdin.

I kept getting phone calls saying, 'I saw you with Ronnie the other day in your black Mini.' – when I hadn't been with him. And anonymous phone calls saying he was seeing another woman.

When I challenged him about the calls, he dismissed it as usual. 'Don't be dozy, Bar, it's the police trying to wind us up.' When I asked him about a blue mascara brush and lipstick I'd found in the car, he said they belonged to barmaids he'd taken home in the car late at night. The funny thing was all these barmaids seemed to wear the same perfume because the car always reeked of it.

It was almost as if he wanted me to find out. I may be deceiving myself, even all these years later, but Ronnie is a very weak person, and I think that he'd got into someone else's clutches, and part of him at least wanted me to rescue him. I've always had a relaxed view of infidelity: if it was just that he was giving her one, then I wouldn't have minded – I was hardly in a position to throw stones. But what was important to me was that we should both be honest. I wanted us to sit down and thrash it all out. So much evidence now weighed against him, I wanted to know precisely where I stood. But Ronnie has a horror of honesty.

I took the advice of my solicitor who suggested a private detective. I was a bit cagey about this at first because of what might crawl out of the woodwork. You could never tell with someone as secretive as Ronnie. But in the end I thought, Sod 'im, and went ahead.

A couple of weeks later the detective agency called me backstage at Nottingham. They couldn't have picked a worse time. I was about to go on stage, the tannoy was blaring out, dressers were charging around, there was a general state of chaos.

'Miss Windsor? Is it convenient to talk?'

'Well not really, but go on.'

'Your husband has been going to a flat in Edgware four times in one week.'

Not bloody Edgware! Now I knew why he didn't want to buy that house in Windsor. The detective told me the girl's name was Susan Haylock, the same name I was given by the reporter in Blackpool. I felt sick and dizzy as I hung up the phone. Then I thought of Dickie Henderson's advice: the show must go on. I composed myself, held my head up and waited for my entrance.

'Hello everybody. My name's Aladdin!'

'Have you anything to tell me, Ronnie?'
'What do you mean?'
'Are you doing anything you shouldn't?'
He shrugged his shoulders and looked perplexed.
'Are you sure, because people always want to tell you things, bad things. What I'm trying to say is that I get the odd phone call saying you're doing silly things, and that there might be someone else.'
'Don't be daft! After all you did for me? You're my life!'

He must have thought I was a fool. He persisted in denying the affair. He even thought up some silly excuse when I said he'd been seen going in and out of a flat.

I was getting nowhere, once again, so I tried a different line – the sympathetic one. He'd been through so much with the trial and the Press. It was nobody's fault our marriage had broken down. I didn't blame him for looking around, and so on. I might have saved my breath. Still he denied there was anyone else.

I was at a loss to know how to force it out of him. In the end I decided to let the affair burn itself out. I just got on with my show.

One weekend my understudy picked me up in Edgware to take me back to Nottingham. Before we got on to the M1 she stopped for petrol and whose red Honda should I see pulling up opposite the petrol station but Ronnie's. He spotted me, too, jumped out of his car and ran towards me. 'I suppose you're meeting someone,' he said. 'Going back to Nottingham with some guy?' It was crazy, he was twisting things to make it look like I was in the wrong.

It all came to a head one Bank Holiday Monday. I was at home watching the film *Sayonara* on the box. Ronnie appeared, all dressed up, at 10.30 in the morning. He said he was off to a club. After he'd gone, it occurred to me that no club would be open on a Bank Holiday. I knew where he was off to, alright! I called a cab, threw some clothes on and headed for Susan Haylock's address, given to me by the detective agency.

I told the cabbie I wanted to see if there were any flats for sale. I looked for the red Honda but couldn't see it in front of the flats where she lived. I was very relieved, but as soon as the taxi reversed by the side of the building to leave my heart missed a beat – sticking out of the courtyard was the tail of a red Honda, unmistakably Ronnie's. I ran round to the entrance, then realized I didn't know the number of Haylock's flat. I pressed some of the entry-phone buttons, but nothing happened. When a young man came along, I immediately switched on the actress and said, 'Oh, thank God, I'm visiting my girlfriend . . . I have a key to her flat but not one for the main entrance.'

'That's all right, love, I'll let you in!'

Now what? I can't go knocking on every door. I ran along the ground floor, up to the first floor and then I spied a door opening, and was about to ask where Miss Haylock lived, when I stopped frozen in my tracks. Coming out of the flat were Ronnie, Susan Haylock, an older lady, whom I took to be her mother, and a child.

I'd come prepared to catch them, but it shook me all the same. Ronnie blanched when he saw me.

'This is Tommy Haylock's missus,' he mumbled. 'I'm doing her a favour . . .'

'Yeah! Don't you bloody lie to me!'

Sue Haylock stood there, looking smug, as if to say, 'I'm pleased you've seen us together with your own eyes.'

I stared at her unblinkingly. I noticed that her mascara was blue. I could see how people mistook her for me. They say imitation is the best form of flattery. Her blonde hair was done in exactly the same style as mine. The big difference now, though, was that she was all tarted up and I was looking more like a bag lady.

'Now I know who you are,' I said to her. 'The last time I saw you, you were serving me a drink.'

I began shouting at Ronnie and throwing punches. The old girl looked frightened.

'Stop it, Bar, you're showing me up!' Ronnie pushed me away. 'Come on, let's get out of here.'

'I'll bloody kill you!' I said to Ronnie when we got outside. In the courtyard beside his Honda was this black Mini, just like mine. For some reason Sue Haylock started running towards it. Perhaps she panicked, I don't know, but it made me see red and I gave chase, bringing her to the ground. I suppose anyone watching would have been reminded irresistibly of the fight scenes in *Carry On Camping* and *Carry On Girls*. I just tore at her, raising my head once or twice to apologize to her mother. My fury wasn't so much because she'd been having it off with my old man as that she had stood by and let him take a beating that night in Ruislip. The insurance lady at Heathrow had told me that she had just stood there screaming. She never lifted a finger to help him, even when he was bleeding all over the floor.

Ronnie was terrified by all this. He didn't know what to do. He tried to pull me off but he couldn't wrench us apart. In the end I said to him, 'Right, get in that car!'

He paid off the taxi, who must have got a right old eyeful, and Sue Haylock roared off in the black Mini.

'Right you,' I said when we were in the Honda. 'You've got some explaining to do. So you think I've gone off my rocker, do you? Phone calls, lipstick, bikinis in our villa . . . all these bloody lies. Now I've found you out! You're going to tell me everything . . . and in front of your brother Jimmy.'

When we got to Jimmy's I started shouting at him again: 'Take a look at your arse'ole of a brother! I've just caught him red-handed with this girl. He's nothing but a dirty slag!'

'She's just a friend,' Ronnie whimpered.

'After all Bar's been through for you,' Jimmy said. 'You're a silly bugger, Ronnie, really you are.'

It did a power of good getting rid of all those pent-up feelings and frustrations. The questions, the doubts, and finally the anger had been eating away at me for far too long. It wasn't all out of my system by any means. I was still fuming when we got home. I looked at Ronnie with hatred in my eyes. 'That's it. Now you're going.'

'You don't mean it?'

'I do, you're out. I don't want to see you again. I don't want anything to do with you.'

'But it's not what you think it is.' He kept on protesting as I charged up the stairs. I grabbed all his clothes out of the wardrobes and drawers: shirts, ties, socks, suits.

'Windsor, you can't do this, Windsor, please!'

But I took no notice. Remembering what my father used to do with Mummy's clothes during a fight, I chucked the whole lot out of the window. And as it fell to the ground below, it struck me that everything matched.

9

For a week Ronnie phoned me every night begged me to let him come home. Each time I said 'No', out came the same old story:

'Listen to me, Bar. Sue Haylock's old man is in the nick. I promised him I'd look after her. You don't want me to go back on my word, do you?'

Calling him a liar, and worse, made no difference. He still said I was accusing him wrongly. It was the story of Ronnie's life!

Then he suddenly stopped phoning. He knew I'd start worrying if there was no word from him. I began to think his enemies had finally got him, that he might be propping up a bridge somewhere. I made enquiries. Then I heard he'd taken off for Spain.

In the war of nerves Ronnie was winning. For three days I sat in an armchair unable to move and unwilling to speak to anyone. I never washed, combed my hair or ate anything.

Eventually, he phoned. 'You wanted me?'

'Why haven't you been in touch?'

'You didn't want me, did you?'

Then I realized that throwing him out was hurting me more than it was hurting him.

He said: 'I've run out of clothes and I'm coming home to get some more.'

I was sedated with Valium when he turned up. Quite out of character he came straight over and put his arms round me. He said he wanted his £50,000 share of the sale of the house. When he tried to kiss me, I picked the phone up and threw it at him.

'What's wrong, Bar? What's got into you?'

He made it seem as if everything that had happened a week or so earlier was just a figment of my imagination. I felt too tired, too weak to fight it.

He moved back in. But the lies, the deceit, and the fight with Haylock, had all taken their toll. I started getting bad stomach pain. I thought I had cancer. Ronnie said he would take me to hospital for some tests. He stayed by my side the whole time, making it really difficult for me to hate him.

On the way home he said, 'Why don't we stop off at an estate agents and see if we can find somewhere nice to live. You've always fancied a garden flat, haven't you?' It was true that since the robbery I'd felt a bit nervy in the house on my own. So I welcomed a move, but only if Ronnie really felt the same way.

In the next three weeks Ronnie fussed over me like a mother hen, and it was clear he was trying to get back into my good books. Then I started to get mysterious phone calls: as soon as I answered, the receiver would be replaced.

One day I came across a letter on Ronnie's pillow. It

was as if he had left it there on purpose for me to find while I was doing the housework. This letter was to Ronnie from Sue, contained nothing but threats. Evidently they'd had a terrible row and now she intended telling all to the newspapers. How could there be any real love between them if she had to resort to these tactics to get him back? I'd never do a thing like that, no matter what happened, and Ronnie knew it. I left the letter exactly where it was, on the bed, and said nothing. Ronnie was in a mess and couldn't handle it. In my present state neither could I. The feeling of sickness in my stomach redoubled.

We moved to a penthouse flat at Hendon Hall Court where we'd started our married life. We'd always fancied the top floor, the penthouse, and now we could afford it. A week before the move we went to lunch with the porter, Wayne, and his wife Jean. During the meal Ronnie's eyes filled with tears.

'This is what I want,' he said. Wayne and Jean looked a bit nonplussed. We all stared down at our roast potatoes and tried to change the subject. Then, as if there were a lot of turmoil inside, he said: 'This is it, this is our life, just me and my Bar.'

It was spring 1982. I set to work on designing our new apartment. We had a tidy sum in the bank from the sale of our home in Stanmore, which was enough for me to buy new furniture and fabrics.

Ronnie had had to sell the club, and now he was at a loose end. I knew Ronnie could earn a crust, but he was always better at spending it. I was also worried about how he might set about earning. He hated being short of money, and I was worried he'd do something silly. I said: 'Don't ever tell me anything. The day might come when I hate you so much . . .'

We were also under pressure from Ronnie's brother, Johnny, who'd just come out of a bitter divorce, and wanted to sell his share of our Spanish villa. Apparently, Johnny's new wife preferred to go elsewhere on holiday. I was against the idea. Okay, the villa was cheap to run and he loved going there, but it was only occupied three months of the year. We didn't need the hassle of owning it lock, stock and barrel. Not for the first time, however, I gave in; Johnny had been especially good to me during the trial, so I owed him a favour.

While I was doing a national tour of *The Mating Game*, Ronnie spent a lot of time in Spain. He said he was doing up the villa.

I really felt the strain of doing *The Mating Game* after six months without a break. In the last week I began feeling sick and at one performance, they had to bring the curtain down. The doctor diagnosed 'nervous panic' and this storm hit the headlines, even appearing on *News at Ten*. Now I couldn't even be ill in private! After all my troubles with Ronnie, I'd lost a hell of a lot of self-belief. I was losing Ronnie, and was worried I couldn't ever do my job well on stage again.

I felt very old and very unloved.

Ronnie read about my collapse and came rushing back from Spain. He took me back to the villa to recuperate. I was surprised to find he *had* been doing DIY around the place, improving the kitchen and installing a TV. It seemed to me he was making it into a proper home. 'That's because I'm spending more time over here,' he said.

Panto beckoned once again and I returned to Oxford for *Aladdin* with Keith Harris. Ronnie was away for the whole panto season, apparently making further improvements to the villa.

At the end of the season I went back to the flat in Edgware, as did Ronnie. But I began to think I was going off my rocker. I kept thinking I could see Susan Haylock. If I went to the chemist, she was lurking behind the cosmetics. If I went to my favourite boutique to try on some dresses, up popped this face, with the blonde hair, watching me. The minute I'd see her she would disappear. I saw her once driving past Hendon Hall Court and at other times, as I drove in, she'd be driving out. It went on all the time. When I told Ronnie, he just said I was imagining things. He reminded me that without my glasses I can't see very well. But I saw all the proof I needed at my health club one evening. I waited until the phantom was out of the way, then asked the attendant if he knew the girl's identity. He checked in his visitors' book. Sure enough it was Sue Haylock. All I felt was relief to know I hadn't actually flipped my lid. When I tackled Ronnie about it, all he said was: 'I can't stop her going places, can I?'

Haylock's continual presence over several months, like some ghostly apparition, caused me great distress. Obviously she lived nearby. My biggest fear was that Ronnie had set her up somewhere.

In my heart, though, I knew the fight to keep my husband was a lost cause. Sue Haylock had set her cap at Ronnie. She was determined to win him and, being away on tour so much I was in no position to take her on. Besides, being as ill as I was, I didn't have the energy or desire to see it to the death. Presumably this malicious game of peek-a-boo was her way of telling me she was the victor.

Ronnie and I went to the villa again in the spring of 1983 before rehearsals began for a summer season at Scarborough, where I was booked to do *The Mating Game* yet again – in my sick and nervous state I could only tackle scripts I already knew very well. My cousin Roy turned up at the villa with his family. After a meal out, we fancied a bit of night life so Ronnie suggested going to a friend's club.

We were watching my cousin's daughter dancing at the club when I heard the owner say, 'Hello, look who's just walked in!'

I followed Ronnie's startled gaze to the entrance where a noisy, frizzy-haired blonde, dressed entirely in white, was making her presence felt. Ronnie, very agitated by now, turned to me. 'Don't start, Bar, don't start.'

'It's all right, I'm with my family. I won't embarrass you!'

I cut short my stay, knowing this would probably be my last visit to the villa. On the plane home alone it all seemed so unnecessary. If only Ronnie had been man enough to own up to his infidelities I could have forgiven him. On my side I'd never have been unfaithful to Ronnie with anyone, even Thomas Powell, if Ronnie had been strong, and shown he wanted me. I desperately tried to fit in with Ronnie – I did all I could for him – but he would never fit in with my life style or do what I wanted.

Perhaps the real crux of the matter was that Ronnie never liked show business. A lot of the time he saw it as a rival. The profession took me away from him. Showbiz with all its glitz and glamour was so much a part of me I could never settle for just being a mousey little housewife. Ronnie is an old-fashioned man who wants someone with him all the time, someone always at his beck and call to cook his meals and clean his socks but he reserves the right to do his own thing when he wants to. He also needs someone to look after him in the sense of making all the decisions. He wants a quiet and easy life: 'Leave it all to Bar,' he always used to say. But I don't think he ever understood how much his trial and all that surrounded it had changed me. I could no longer give him what I always had done – what Sue Haylock was now offering.

All the time he was in Spain, Ronnie phoned me regular as clockwork every Saturday morning. We talked about trivialities, then during one of these calls I found myself saying: 'Ronnie, darling, I know it's all over between us. I think we ought to get a divorce.' The words just slipped out. I was shocked that I had taken the initiative, yet deep down in my heart I knew it was the right decision.

The boarding house, once owned by my Uncle Digger and Aunty Margaret, was bang opposite the Floral Hall, Scarborough, where I was appearing in *The Mating Game* for the umpteenth time. Scarborough brought back a flood of childhood memories: this was where I'd once told the singer Lita Rosa how much I wanted to learn to sing and dance. Thirty years on little Barbara-Ann Deeks was starring there.

I should have felt on top of the world and it probably appeared that I was to the rest of the cast. But inside I felt sad and lonely. Ronnie continued to call me every Saturday morning as if I'd never mentioned the divorce.

I went to parties without enjoying them. At one I was introduced to a young man called Stephen Hollings, who, I was told, was dying to meet me. Thoughts of another man, let alone a handsome young one, never entered my head. Stephen could only have been in his mid-twenties. Once he was pointed out to me I realized I'd seen him at a number of other town functions. Stephen was tall, slim and very handsome. He reminded me of Ronnie's younger brother, David, and, like Ronnie he was immaculately dressed and groomed. His eyes seemed to light up when we met, and once in conversation we discovered all the things we had in common. By the end of the evening I felt I had to get to know him better, but common sense told me it would not be wise. The world and his wife knew I was still married to Ronnie Knight.

It wasn't hard to find out more about Stephen because he was a popular figure around the town. He was manager of The Corner, a busy leisure centre in Peaseholm Park, something of a local landmark, which explained why I'd seen him at public functions. A few days later at the Grand Hotel, seeing my old mate Ronnie Hilton in cabaret, I came face to face with Stephen unexpectedly and it just confirmed my first impression – I fancied the pants off him!

At the end of the evening he took me back to the flat I shared with actress Carol Ann Darock and we slept together for the first time – when I'm smitten with someone I don't wait for invitations, I go for it like a bull in a china shop! Next morning I rushed straight round to The Corner.

'I don't know what I'm doing here . . . . I just had to see you again!'

Stephen said he felt the same. Then he said a lovely thing: 'You look so pretty without all that stage make-up.'

I next saw Stephen a fortnight later at a Butlin's birthday party in my honour, their way of repaying me for charity work I'd done for them during the run of *The Mating Game*. All the artists from the neighbouring summer shows were there, including Cannon and Ball. It was a total surprise and made all the more special by the presence of my handsome young lover.

We began to see each other regularly and our affair attracted a lot of tittle-tattle. I suppose it was inevitable, given my record, that I would soon discover he was engaged to be married to a local girl in six weeks' time.

I was knocked out by his reaction when I challenged him: 'I don't want to get married. I feel as if I'm being pushed into it. I shouldn't be getting married feeling as I do about you.' He explained that his intended, a local waitress called Lorraine Nicklin, had been his steady girlfriend for some time. They'd broken up once and got back together again. Now both families expected them to marry.

Fed up with people asking where Ronnie was, I started divorce proceedings, and the Press prepared to send in the clowns. When Rosalie Shann of the *News of the World* called, I thought it was a good chance to tell the world that my marriage to Ronnie was over. That way I would feel much better when I was seen around with Stephen – no tut-tutting, no raised eyebrows. I told her I wanted to be free to love again. I said nothing about Stephen personally but they were just determined to find out the identity of my new lover. Stephen told me he was going to let his parents know about our liaison. He said he had made up his mind to tell Lorraine.

But the story broke too quickly. Before Stephen had a chance to tell his folks or his girlfriend, a picture of us together, taken at my Butlin's birthday party, was splashed across the tabloids.

The Press descended on his parents' house and pestered poor Lorraine. They were even crawling about The Corner where Stephen worked. When we talked about it, I told him to deny everything. 'I didn't realize you were *that* famous,' he said. Stephen was so confused he even told some reporters he was going ahead with his marriage to Lorraine. It is bad enough for someone like me having to face the Press. It must have been terrifying for Stephen who had never been in the limelight in his life.

It was time for Windsor to be sensible and grown up for once in her life: 'I'll go back to London and we'll see what happens.' I could hardly get the words out. 'I know what you're going through, darling. You know you've got my love.'

So when the Scarborough season finished, there was nothing else for it but to return to London alone. I missed Stephen and I believed he must be feeling the same. The first thing I had to do was break away from Hendon, a place of too many painful memories. I found a lovely house in Swiss Cottage and moved there in November 1984. My accountant, Albert Fox, said I could just afford it. Without Albert I'm sure I would have landed in the gutter by now!

Ronnie came to see my new place and brought up the subject of divorce. He said he thought we should leave it a couple of years. It obviously didn't suit him to get on with it and I was in no state to press it. Besides I no longer knew what was happening with Stephen.

Meanwhile, the producer Mark Furness, for whom I had done the Scarborough season, booked me for an extensive tour of the comedy, *Rattle of a Simple Man*, playing opposite Geoffrey Hughes of *Coronation Street*. When the script arrived, I couldn't believe what I'd taken on. Every time I looked at all the lines I had to learn, I felt sick and panicky and the words became jumbled in front of my eyes. Behind it was all the anxiety about my personal life. Stephen was gone and for the first time in my life I had to cope without Ronnie. I knew I was in danger of cracking up again. The *Sunday Express* did an article on me in a series called 'Things I Wish I'd Known At 18'. Two days after taking my photograph they rang me up: 'Barbara, this picture is just awful. We're going to have to do another photo session.' I told them, 'No, that's how I look now!' I went to a health farm to pull myself together for the sake of the tour, but I just couldn't. There was nothing else for it. I had to tell my agent, Richard Stone, I couldn't cope with *Rattle of a Simple Man*.

The only work I could cope with was stuff I could do on automatic pilot – so it was back to pantomime.

I heard nothing from Stephen Hollings until the first week of *Aladdin* at Chichester in December. I'd thought about him constantly in the four months since I'd left Scarborough. He said he wanted to see me, so I made arrangements for him to come to Chichester. I waited for him but he never showed up. No letter, no phone call, nothing. I sent him a Christmas card but received none in return.

I came home after the panto broken-hearted, with only the occasional visit from Ronnie to lift my spirits.

On 21 January 1984, the day after his birthday, Ronnie turned up really hung over. He hadn't recovered from the previous day's celebrations. I felt like Ronnie looked – a wreck! To add to my problems I had a flu virus and was meant to be doing a personal appearance in Brighton. Ronnie urged me not to go, but I told him I needed the money.

Next day there was a message to say that Ronnie had phoned in a state. I had no idea where he was so I couldn't contact him, but in the evening he called again and this time I was home.

'I'm over here,' he said.

'Over where?'

'Y'know, the villa.'

I was gob-smacked. Only the day before I'd seen him at Swiss Cottage.

'The Old Bill are after me. They've picked up Johnny and Jimmy. They're after us for the Security Express job.'

It was a couple of months before it came out in the Press that Ronnie and his brothers, along with an assortment of others, were wanted in connection with the £6 million robbery of a Security Express. I couldn't believe Ronnie was implicated in a robbery of this scale. My thoughts went straight back to the murder trial. The police hate being made to look stupid. They'd do anything to get their own back on Ronnie. Surely this was yet another frame-up? On the phone it was the same confused and pathetic voice I'd heard four years ago when he was charged with murder. I knew he was safe at the villa because Spain had no extradition treaty with Britain, but as the days passed it sank in that Ronnie would not be calling on me any more. Without being fully aware of it, I'd been clinging on to the hope that he would come back to me.

I began turning jobs down. I just sat up all night playing records and watching videos. Normally I would overcome any obstacle, no matter how immovable: a broken arm, a temperature over a hundred, all my marital traumas . . . nothing had prevented me from working in the past. But the loss of Stephen quickly followed by Ronnie's dramatic exit was more than I could bear.

My friends knew I was someone who could not survive without love in my life. I envied all those women who lived normal married lives with their husbands beside them through the night. The larger-than-life actor Christopher Biggins, put my predicament in a nutshell: 'You need sex, dear. That's what's wrong with you!' Biggins took me in hand. He seemed to know more about what I wanted than I did. He introduced me to a couple of guys, but I didn't click with either of them. I couldn't relax. One of the things about Stephen was that he didn't give a monkey's for my reputation. Because he'd never even seen a *Carry On* film, I knew he liked me for myself. That's always been a problem for me with men: knowing who wants me for myself and who wants me because I'm bubbly Barbara Windsor with the big boobs!

Thinking of Stephen only dragged me down. I felt I wanted to go to sleep and never wake up. In the midst of this gloom I found myself writing a long letter to my father, whom I hadn't seen for years. I must have been desperate for comfort and words of kindness, but I could never have predicted his response. I hoped the special bond between father and daughter would be strong enough to heal old wounds.

Daddy called me, his tone far from conciliatory:
'What do you want?'

'I just wanted to talk to you . . .'

He didn't let me finish the sentence, launching into a
tirade of accusations, recriminations and demands.
Nothing I said made any difference. He ranted on at me
the way he used to go on at Mummy. He was clearly
determined to upset me.

I wasn't doing anything intentionally to provoke his
anger, neither had I as a child. Why couldn't a man of his
intelligence see that I was an innocent victim of my
parents' incompatibility? Without saying a word, I
gently replaced the receiver. I was crying as I did so, but
there seemed no point in contacting him again.

Barbara Windsor had hit rock bottom.

Amid all the gloom I received a phone call from Davy
Kaye of the Water Rats, the showbiz charity organiza-
tion, asking me if I would help raise money for them.

'I'm sorry, Davy, I just couldn't face it at the
moment.'

'Blimey, you are feeling sorry for yourself,' he said.

'I don't want to go out,' I began crying down the
phone: 'I haven't been out for ages.'

Davy was so kind and sympathetic that I finished up
agreeing to do his charity work, and the joke was that it
turned out to be more of a favour to me than anyone else.
All my little problems paled in comparison to the ones I
was finding out about. I've learnt such a lot in my work
for the Lady Ratlings, the women's wing of the Water
Rats. I've involved myself in the problems of elderly
people dying of hypothermia, children in need, the
physically and mentally handicapped. After that sort of

experience you say to yourself, 'How dare you sit at home and wallow in self pity?' The more you think of others the less you worry about yourself.

Ronnie rang me more than once to ask me not to go ahead with divorce proceedings. I still loved him but I had to face the facts – Ronnie could survive without me, so I had to learn to survive without him.

Stephen Hollings came back into my life in March 1984.

'What happened last time?' I asked him when he finally called me. Stephen said that after Scarborough, he'd been terrified of the Press. He'd started to believe all I ever wanted was publicity. That's why he got cold feet and shunned me. I sympathized with him totally. If you are the kind of person beloved of the tabloid press, it's natural for people to assume you spend your life chasing after column inches. Stephen told me of the turmoil he'd been in during the past six months, how most evenings he'd been going out to get pissed. He'd taken off for Ibiza for a few weeks to try and sort himself out. While he was there another English tourist came up to him in a bar and said, 'Let me shake hands with the man who's groped Barbara Windsor!' Little did people know that in private I was a complete wreck, and that Stephen literally had to nurse me.

We made plans for him to come and see me that Saturday. He was anxious about attracting any more Press attention, so we agreed he should pose as my hairdresser if anyone asked us any questions while we were having an intimate dinner.

We agreed to meet at the barrier on the station platform, but when he arrived he walked straight past me,

'What are you playing at?' I yelled, running after him.

'Sssh! Sssh!' he said. 'The Press might be here.' Stephen is basically an uncomplicated Yorkshire lad. The small community of Malton, where he was brought up, is light years away from the ballyhoo of London and the life I led.

Stephen told me his parents and grandparents were against the match. Quite naturally they felt protective towards their son. They had only seen me on television and knew I was almost twice Stephen's age and unlikely to bear him any children. His fiancée Lorraine, on the other hand, was a nice Yorkshire girl with every prospect of becoming a loyal wife and mother. I understood the field of conflict all too well. But when I realized, as I did that evening, that we would always be together, then it was up to me to prove to his family that my interest in their son was genuine and heartfelt.

We behaved very properly in the restaurant, and talked a lot of things over. When we got up to go, a bit pissed by this time, my bogus hairdresser took a red rose from one of the tables and handed it to me.

'I love you,' he said for all to hear. Then he swept me off my feet and kissed me!

'You idiot,' I screamed. 'Now everybody will know!'

'I don't care.' He smiled broadly at everyone. 'I want the whole world to know I love you.'

It took a long time for me to grasp the fact that Stephen was back in my life. But when I did the old Windsor bounce and bubble came gushing back. I felt confident enough to accept a summer season, especially as it was *The Mating Game* again. What's more it would be in Jersey, an idyllic place for romance! And why not? I felt like a teenager again for the first time in years.

I phoned Ronnie to say I would be coming over to Spain for him to sign the divorce papers.

'I won't be at the villa,' he said, 'I've let it out to a Dutch couple. I'll be staying in Estapona.'

'Ronnie,' I said, 'you don't have to move out of your villa. I know you're with Sue Haylock and it's okay.'

'I'm not with anyone.'

'Why are you so paranoid about it?'

'I'm trying to sort out my life,' he replied.

It was plain that I couldn't go to the villa, so I asked a friend, who owned a property nearby if I could stay with her. That's where Ronnie came to see me. Knowing how smartly Ronnie always dressed I wore a lemon turban, lemon shorts and top, and gold shoes. I couldn't believe it at first when he turned up in a dirty tracksuit. Then I guessed why: he didn't want Haylock to know he was seeing me, so he used the excuse of going for a run.

Ronnie tried to postpone the divorce yet again. I could tell he was feeling insecure, a fugitive from justice living with a woman who might walk out on him at any moment. I tried to reassure him that my reasons had nothing to do with his present situation. 'If you're worried I might testify against you, forget it,' I told him. 'I don't hate you. I care about you. I've spent 20 years with you and I only want to remember the good times. Would I do anything to destroy you?'

I saw Ronnie three times on that trip. On the last occasion we went out to dinner and had a wonderful time. Now he was immaculately dressed. I told him how Stephen and I were together again and that was why I wanted the divorce.

'Is he the one who didn't want you once the pressure was on?' he asked.

'That's unfair. Remember when it first happened to you? You're used to it now.'

Stephen phoned me every day from Scarborough. When I returned from Spain with the divorce papers signed, he had already given in his notice, and sold his car and bungalow. Within a week he was on my doorstep with all his bits and pieces. Life was going to be so different from now on.

Before leaving for Jersey we issued a press release with a photograph of ourselves, thinking it might help get them off our backs. 'My life is an open book,' I warned Stephen: 'I won't be able to hide you. You'll have to be prepared to be called a toy boy and all the rest of it.' In the event, some very nice articles appeared.

The four-month season in Jersey gave us a chance to really get to know each other. It was a kind of trial marriage. We rented a house on the seafront from Billy Walker, the ex-boxer. Stephen drove me to the theatre and cooked for us. It didn't take me long to realize that I was now in the company of a real chef – he always managed to use *every* pan in the kitchen and made enough gravy for fifty people.

While we were in Jersey, I tried to sort out financial affairs with Ronnie once and for all. He said he was going to sell the villa and give me my share – I knew I'd have to wait a long time. One day he rang:

'Hello, it's me.'

'Hello, Ron.'

'I'm in 'ospital.' It turned out he'd had an operation on his back. He said, 'I don't suppose, I mean, I expect you've blown me out of your Private Pension Plan?'

I said I hadn't.

'Can I have the number?' he said.

'Well can I come over?'

'No, just give me the number,' he said.

Then together with Albert Fox, my accountant, I tried to see how I could help him with other financial matters.

I used to leave messages for Ronnie at a bar in Spain until Albert asked why I wasn't phoning him at the villa.

'He's not on the phone,' I said.

'Of course he is.' Albert then made Ronnie give me his number.

I ask you, what on earth was the point of lying about Haylock at this stage in the game?

Ronnie wanted to prepare his defence in case he was brought back to England. Again he sought my help. I asked why Sue Haylock couldn't do it. He said, 'You've got more idea . . . you know the routine.'

I was loath to get involved in Ronnie's legal troubles again because it was unfair to Stephen. I never thought he'd put up with it, and who could blame him? But he was terrific. 'He trusts you more than anyone else,' Stephen said. 'The man obviously feels his hands are tied in Spain, and he knows you'll help him find a solicitor who will take care of things.'

When Ronnie's brothers finally came to trial for the Security Express job, I appeared as a witness for Johnny at the Old Bailey. Ronnie talked me into it. It was the last place on earth I wanted to be, but I told the court how I had paid money over for Johnny's share of the villa. A lot of good it did him! He went down for twenty-two years for the robbery, while Jimmy got eight years for receiving.

But Sue Haylock's behaviour was what hurt more than anything. Interviewed by a newspaper, she had a go at Stephen and me. She described me as being desperate and only going out with him because I couldn't find anyone else. After I brought the subject up with Ronnie, she wrote to me saying how sorry she was and how she hoped we would be friends one day. But the article spoiled any chance we had of becoming friends – which was a shame because Ronnie and Stephen got on well. Ronnie told Stephen: 'Look after Bar, she's yours now.' – she's a wonderful lady.'

Ronnie seemed to accept the idea of me being with someone so much younger. Most people had a problem with it, including me. 'Cor blimey,' I said to my friend, Anna Karen, 'in 20 years' time, when I'm 60 something, Stephen will still be in his 40s!' But Jersey proved one thing. It might sound daft, but when you're deeply in love and happy with someone, age doesn't come into it. Stephen is even less concerned about the age gap than I am and it's never been the cause of arguments between us. That's not to say we don't have arguments. I've had more rows with Stephen in six years than I ever had with Ronnie in twenty, because Stephen is such a strong character. He's a real Yorkshireman, and he won't always back down when I want him to.

He is also used to working hard for his money. He is a connoisseur of wine and a qualified chef, specializing in French cuisine, and his ambition was to run a country pub or restaurant. He didn't like being unoccupied while we were in Jersey, laying himself open to taunts of being a toy boy. I wanted to help Stephen find a place of his own in the country and so we put both our houses on the market.

I played Dick Whittington in Dartford that season, which gave Stephen and I plenty of time to drive around Berkshire and Buckinghamshire looking at pubs and restaurants on the market.

On Christmas Eve Stephen took me to Peter's restaurant in Swiss Cottage. Over a candlelit meal he produced a fabulous heart-shaped diamond ring and proposed to me. I knew what was coming and Stephen had the devil's own job to make me behave. I'm terrible like that. I love the fact that he's romantic but I get this irresistible urge to giggle.

When my divorce did finally come through at the beginning of January 1985, Stephen and I started to make wedding plans. This time I wanted something special. Until my dying day I shall never forget being married to Ronnie in a register office in the pouring rain, knowing I might be called on to the *Carry On* set at any minute.

We were still looking for a place for Stephen when I went into summer season at Butlin's in Minehead. The show was called *A Right Carry On*. By the end of the end of the seventy-six week season, we'd found exactly the place we'd been searching for – a 300-year-old pub with a restaurant attached in Amersham, Bucks, called the Plough Inn; oddly enough it used to be a furniture factory making Windsor chairs. The only problem was fitting all my furniture into the small flat above the pub that was to be our accommodation. An adjacent flat would be occupied by Stephen's brother, Stuart, and his wife Jean, who would help us run it.

The night we took over I mentioned our new venture on *Wogan* and when I got back to Amersham there were people queuing to get in, despite the fact it was pouring with rain. It must be the only time anyone has plugged a pub on Terry's show!

Stephen's mother, Pat, told the Press: 'If my son wants to become a star, then good for him.' It was important to me that we should have her blessing as well as that of Stephen's father Frank, a very good man. I needed to know that his family were now firmly behind us. I also decided to tell Ronnie of our wedding plans and assured him it would be a quiet affair.

I'd seen an advertisement in the paper for 'Weddings in Paradise' at the Ocho Rios resort in Jamaica. It seemed to be the perfect answer for Stephen and me to travel far afield, and so avoid the media circus.

It only remained for me to find an outfit. The one I chose from a favourite shop in Marylebone High Street was ankle-length with a high scalloped neckline at the front continuing down the back in a deep V to the waist. It was made of delicate ivory lace embroidered with lovers' knots. The tiniest peach-seed pearls formed little flowers over the palest of peach satin. When I showed it to Stephen I burst into tears: 'I've bought a white wedding dress. I'll look ridiculous.'

'Don't be silly,' said Stephen. 'If that's what you want, it'll be lovely.'

'I wish Mummy could've seen it,' I said.

Our wedding day would be 12 April 1986, which was also the date of Stephen's grandparents' golden wedding. Travelling on the plane to Jamaica with us would be one Press photographer, Arthur Steele from the *Sun*. We decided to give them an exclusive, so the other papers would leave us in peace. Arthur was quiet, discreet and happy to give us the privacy we wanted.

From the moment we touched down in Jamaica we were treated like gods, because everyone knew me from the *Carry Ons*. In the five days' holiday we had before the wedding, Stephen and Arthur spent a lot of time swimming, but because of my fair complexion I stayed in the apartment in the heat of the day. I didn't want to be married with a blistering red mush! I tried to persuade Stephen to keep out of the sun, too, but he does what he wants to do. He was swimming out at sea an hour before our wedding. Our balcony overlooked the beach, and I was standing there in my rollers shouting: 'Git your arse back 'ere!' He laughed, waved and swam further out to sea.

The holiday company had arranged for a minister to conduct the service. We needed two witnesses, so I asked a lady from Nottingham who was on the same flight as us and the hotel chef – an appropriate choice, I thought. We were married by a black Salvation Army minister at four o'clock in the afternoon. Stephen looked so handsome in a blue Yves St Laurent suit he'd bought in Jersey. It was the happiest moment of my life.

I didn't have a chance to see the wedding cake I'd very carefully ordered before the ceremony, and Arthur Steele's disparaging remarks didn't prepare me for a close encounter with the monstrosity that awaited us on the beach, where the reception was to be held. As Stephen and I approached the tables where food had been laid out, it stood out like a flashing beacon. It wasn't so much the pale apricot I'd asked for as traffic-light orange. Nobody could face eating it, so we did the conventional thing of appearing to cut it for the photographs, and left it at that, while the minister made us sing 'The Lord is My Shepherd' – more usually heard at funerals! I never know whether my life is closer to a *Carry On* or to a play by Joe Orton.

Next day, when we went to the airport to begin our return journey, we found that the dreaded cake had been packed up as part of our hand luggage. Minutes after we checked in there was a power failure at the airport, which meant that we were not only plunged into darkness but, in sweltering heat, bereft of any air conditioning. We could barely see each other let alone the other passengers, most of whom were black. What I found most scary were these disembodied white things that appeared to be floating through the air. It wasn't until a shaft of moonlight caught the whites of their eyes that I realized it was gleaming white teeth I'd been frightened of! There was a mad scramble for the London flight, the last for many hours, we were told. First-class tickets did not assure us special treatment – in fact we were lucky to get seats at all. As if that wasn't enough hassle, the icing on the cake had melted, smothering seats, baggage and Stephen's designer suit with this horrible orange gunge. When we got to Heathrow I decided to declare the cake.

'I've just got married in Jamaica and this is my cake,' I said to the customs officer.

'Cake! Are you sure?' he said with a look of disbelief. Convinced there was hash or perhaps even an arms cache concealed inside this gooey mess, he plunged into it with both hands. Well, at least it saved us the trouble of eating it.

10

'What do you think about it . . . were you invited to the wedding . . . how do you get on with Sue Haylock?'

The questions were barked at me by a pack of hungry newshounds outside the Plough Inn on 6 June 1987, the day Ronnie was to marry Sue Haylock in Spain. The Plough is just off the village green in Amershan in the middle of gentle countryside. There are two village shops and the pace of life hasn't changed a lot in 50 years. The sudden invasion of Fleet Street's none-too-sensitive muckrakers was like an SAS squad storming a monastery.

It was made even more embarrassing for me because I had no prior knowledge of Ronnie's marital plans, other than a vague hunch that he and Haylock would eventually tie the knot. I found it unforgivable that Ronnie hadn't let me know the wedding date. Then I could have prepared for the media onslaught.

Swallowing my pride and indignation I phoned Ronnie that night to wish him luck. He was happy and talkative, describing the wedding as 'a small, intimate do'. That sounded very sensible. Only a fool would deliberately provoke the Old Bill by staging some flashy affair.

But when I got the Sunday newspapers next day I couldn't believe my eyes. The wedding was splashed over every tabloid. It looked exactly like that big wedding in *The Godfather* and it allegedly cost Ronnie £60,000. Yet he still hadn't paid me my share of the villa, and, more importantly, so far as the police were concerned, he didn't have that kind of money to throw around. The guest list included all the most-wanted fugitives from Britain living on the Costa del Sol. It was as if they were cocking a snook at the boys from Scotland Yard who'd be watching everything from cars parked nearby.

'I can't stop you,' said Stephen, 'but you'll never forgive yourself.' I ignored him; I made the mistake of giving a series of interviews to the *Sun* in which I found myself offloading a lot of my anger about Ronnie. Up until then I'd only ever said nice things about him to the Press, but my hurt and confusion about the wedding, as well as my fury that he should lay himself open in this way, forced me to speak up. It was so unlike him to make a big spectacle of himself. He'd always been a shy man, staying in the background. My only conclusion was that Sue Haylock had put him up to it.

One thing I was proved right about was the renewal of police interest. Just six weeks after Ronnie's extravaganza they contacted me. I was summoned to Leman Street nick. It must have looked as if I was going voluntarily to the police to talk about Ronnie, which wasn't the case. The Old Bill asked me to give them a rundown of events around the time of the Security Express robbery for which they wanted to question him. I had to produce diaries, but there was nothing in them linking Ronnie to the job.

I was called to Leman Street six times, and they also came to the Plough. From the start they warned me I would find out a lot of hurtful things. How right they were. I never realized how much of a life Ronnie had created with Sue Haylock before they started living together. There were numerous police pictures of Ronnie and Sue leading a life together before the trial. I always thought I knew Ronnie, and it was a terrible shock to find out I never knew him at all. For the first time in my life I felt I had been totally used. Diane, Ronnie's sister-in-law, had always been a good friend – I'd helped look after her when her husband went inside – and she'd always assured me that she and Ronnie didn't talk to each other because she didn't approve of Sue Haylock. How do you think I felt when I saw photographs of her with Haylock, Ronnie and other members of the family, all happy together years earlier? She called me recently to ask what she'd done to upset me, and I told Diane I didn't want to speak to her any more.

While I was giving the police interviews, Ronnie called me, sounding aggressive and upset.

'I hear you've become a fucking grass,' he shouted at me.

Of course I wasn't a grass, I told him. The only reason I was co-operating with the police was because I had no choice. If the police ask to talk to you, you can't refuse. I was disgusted by his threatening tone, like he no longer trusted me. Any bit of love I had for him went out the window with that one phone call.

I realized, too, how glad I was to be free of all that underworld stuff. At the age of fifty you can't cope with the constant threat of the Old Bill coming round and knocking on your door at any moment.

The stress of all this business inevitably took its toll on my health, and my severe stomach pains turned out to be an ulcer. Having agreed, some months earlier, to take part in *It's A Royal Knockout* at Alton Towers, I was relieved to learn that I wouldn't have to dress up as a turnip and mud-wrestle a water buffalo. Not unless Princess Anne dropped out. I'd been warned by my agent to expect a call from Prince Edward, who was organizing the event, but I got myself into a right old state when John said he'd given the Prince my number at the Plough. I know it sounds a bit snobby but I didn't want him to get the wrong impression so I set off for the Plough from London, hoping to get there before the Prince called. What if Wayne answered the phone? He'd think it was someone pulling his leg! But the air of excitement at the Plough told the whole story.

'Prince Edward phoned, don't y'know!'

'Who answered?'

'I did.' Wayne looked as proud as a peacock.

I was to play Lady Knock opposite Rowan Atkinson's Lord Knock on 14 June 1987. All we had to do was preside over the games in fancy dress and look supercilious. There was no question of making prats of ourselves playing stupid games, thank God.

Security was unbelievable. There were shifty-looking men in dark suits lurking behind every bush. You needed a card for this and a card for that wherever you went. The only thing you could do unaccompanied was . . . well, I expect you can guess.

In keeping with my aristocratic role, Stephen and I stayed in the same hotel as the royals. Su Pollard, who was staying up the road with the other commoners, said accusingly, 'What you doin' with all them posh people? You don't speak any better than wot I do!'

Being a *Carry On* veteran I am used to weathering the worst conditions imaginable, so the muddy, rain-soaked field I had to slurp across in my high heels on our rehearsal day didn't bother me in the least. The best fun was watching the horrified expressions on the faces of stars like Mel Smith and John Travolta, as they discovered what they would have to do the following day.

That evening we were whisked off to some restaurant by coach, and Cliff Richard led us all in a right royal sing-along, with Fergie joining in with *We're All Going On A Summer Holiday*, among other Cliff hits. It reminded me of days out to Southend when we were kids.

The weather remained unchanged for the big day but, by a miracle, it actually stopped raining as soon as the TV cameras started to roll. Somebody up there decided to give us a break. We all wanted Prince Edward's team to win because of all the hard work he'd put into it, but it was to Princess Anne that I presented the team award.

I never seem to stop working these days. The *Carry On* films just become more and more popular. A taxi driver was telling me he'd had all of them out on video. 'Mind you,' he said, 'you're all dead now.' But it's nice, too, to have been discovered by a younger audience. I've had fun working with the Pet Shop Boys, the Young Ones, Harry Enfield and Hale and Pace and also appearing at the London Palladium in *Babes in the Wood* – but this time as the fairy godmother rather than the principal boy! Unlike Ronnie, who always carried on his same routine however many concessions I made, Stephen makes every effort to be around, driving me all over the place and taking a keen interest in my work. When we can't be together, he'll call me. Not every day, but every hour!

I'm very proud of the business he has built up. People come from miles around to go to his pub. He's very popular in the village, particulary with the regulars, many of them war veterans. Stephen's very kind to old people – that's why he married me!

Living at the Plough did have one major disadvantage for me – I was on show all the time. After a day's filming or rehearsal, you're not always in the mood to be chatted up by customers, however well-meaning. When I come home and put the key in the door, I need to be Barbara Hollings. Stephen understood. He said: 'You always say Ronnie Knight would never let you live in the West End, so why don't you get a little mews house?' We found one slap bang in the centre of London, not far from where Kenny Williams used to live. I stay there during the week with my dog Bonnie, a gorgeous Llasa Apso, and Stephen commutes. Weekends we're always together at the Plough, unless I'm working.

I believe the more you see of each other the more your love grows. I would never dream of being unfaithful to Stephen. I hate jealousy and I know from bitter experience how easy it is to provoke it. It destroyed my relationship with Ronnie. I used to think: 'If he believes I've done it, I may as well do it!' Stephen on the other hand really cares for me. He puts himself out for me. And he trusts me completely.

The other day a taxi was dropping us off at the mews. He said to Stephen, 'nice to see'er looking so happy'. And I *am* happy. I'm the happiest little bird in the world.

If I'm ever down all I have to do is walk along the street, and the love I get from the public lifts me sky high.

There's only one shadow, and that, of course, is the worry about what is going to happen to Ronnie. I sometimes talk to him on the phone. He sounds bored to death, his mind seems to be puddled with the sun and sangria. Whatever he thinks, I'd never do anything to hurt him. Because of the twenty years together – and I only think of the good times – he'll always be part of me. I want to help him, but I don't know how. The best I can imagine for him is that he spends the rest of his days in Spain.

I only wish I could hope that one day he might be as happy as I am.